The Pelican Shakespeare

General Editors

Stephen Orgel

A. R. Braunmuller

As You Like It

The comedian Tom King (1730–1805), one of the most famous members of Garrick's Drury Lane company, as Touchstone. From Bell's Shakespeare, 1775.

William Shakespeare

As You Like It

EDITED BY FRANCES E. DOLAN

PENGUIN BOOKS

PENGUIN BOOKS

Published by the Penguin Group

Penguin Group (USA) Inc., 375 Hudson Street, New York, New York 10014, U.S.A.
Penguin Group (Canada), 90 Eglinton Avenue East, Suite 700, Toronto,
Ontario, Canada M4P 2Y3 (a division of Pearson Penguin Canada Inc.)
Penguin Books Ltd, 80 Strand, London WC2R 0RL, England
Penguin Ireland, 25 St Stephen's Green, Dublin 2, Ireland (a division of Penguin Books Ltd)
Penguin Group (Australia), 250 Camberwell Road, Camberwell,
Victoria 3124, Australia (a division of Pearson Australia Group Pty Ltd)
Penguin Books India Pvt Ltd, 11 Community Centre, Panchsheel Park,
New Delhi – 110 017, India
Penguin Group (NZ), 67 Apollo Drive, Rosedale, North Shore 0632, New Zealand
(a division of Pearson New Zealand Ltd)
Penguin Books (South Africa) (Pty) Ltd, 24 Sturdee Avenue, Rosebank,
Johannesburg 2196, South Africa

Penguin Books Ltd, Registered Offices: 80 Strand, London WC2R 0RL, England

As You Like It edited by Ralph M. Sargent published in the
United States of America by Penguin Books 1959
Revised edition published 1970
This new edition edited by Frances E. Dolan published 2000

30 29 28 27 26

LIBRARY OF CONGRESS CATALOGING IN PUBLICATION DATA
Shakespeare, William, 1564–1616.
As you like it / William Shakespeare; edited by Frances E. Dolan.
p. cm.—(The Pelican Shakespeare)
ISBN 978-0-14-071471-5
1. Fathers and daughters—Drama. 2. Exiles—Drama. I. Title. II. Series.
PR2803.A2 D65 2000
822.3'3—dc21   00-033627

Printed in the United States of America
Set in Garamond
Designed by Virginia Norey

Contents

Contents

Aldous Huxley

Publisher's Note

IT IS ALMOST half a century since the first volumes of the Pelican Shakespeare appeared under the general editorship of Alfred Harbage. The fact that a new edition, rather than simply a revision, has been undertaken reflects the profound changes textual and critical studies of Shakespeare have undergone in the past twenty years. For the new Pelican series, the texts of the plays and poems have been thoroughly revised in accordance with recent scholarship, and in some cases have been entirely reedited. New introductions and notes have been provided in all the volumes. But the new Shakespeare is also designed as a successor to the original series; the previous editions have been taken into account, and the advice of the previous editors has been solicited where it was feasible to do so.

Certain textual features of the new Pelican Shakespeare should be particularly noted. All lines are numbered that contain a word, phrase, or allusion explained in the glossarial notes. In addition, for convenience, every tenth line is also numbered, in italics when no annotation is indicated. The intrusive and often inaccurate place headings inserted by early editors are omitted (as is becoming standard practice), but for the convenience of those who miss them, an indication of locale now appears as the first item in the annotation of each scene.

In the interest of both elegance and utility, each speech prefix is set in a separate line when the speaker's lines are in verse, except when those words form the second half of a verse line. Thus the verse form of the speech is kept visually intact. What is printed as verse and what is printed as prose has, in general, the authority of the original texts. Departures from the original texts in this regard have only the authority of editorial tradition and the judgment of the Pelican editors; and, in a few instances, are admittedly arbitrary.

The Theatrical World

Economic realities determined the theatrical world in which Shakespeare's plays were written, performed, and received. For centuries in England, the primary theatrical tradition was nonprofessional. Craft guilds (or "mysteries") provided religious drama – mystery plays – as part of the celebration of religious and civic festivals, and schools and universities staged classical and neoclassical drama in both Latin and English as part of their curricula. In these forms, drama was established and socially acceptable. Professional theater, in contrast, existed on the margins of society. The acting companies were itinerant; playhouses could be any available space – the great halls of the aristocracy, town squares, civic halls, inn yards, fair booths, or open fields – and income was sporadic, dependent on the passing of the hat or on the bounty of local patrons. The actors, moreover, were considered little better than vagabonds, constantly in danger of arrest or expulsion.

In the late 1560s and 1570s, however, English professional theater began to gain respectability. Wealthy aristocrats fond of drama – the Lord Admiral, for example, or the Lord Chamberlain – took acting companies under their protection so that the players technically became members of their households and were no longer subject to arrest as homeless or masterless men. Permanent theaters were first built at this time as well, allowing the companies to control and charge for entry to their performances.

Shakespeare's livelihood, and the stunning artistic explosion in which he participated, depended on pragmatic and architectural effort. Professional theater requires ways to restrict access to its offerings; if it does not, and admission fees cannot be charged, the actors do not get paid, the costumes go to a pawnbroker, and there is no such thing as a professional, ongoing theatrical tradition. The answer to that economic need arrived in the late 1560s and 1570s with the creation of the so-called public or amphitheater playhouse. Recent discoveries indicate that the precursor of the Globe playhouse in London (where Shakespeare's mature plays were presented) and the Rose theater (which presented Christopher Marlowe's plays and some of Shakespeare's earliest ones) was the Red Lion theater of 1567. Archaeological studies of the foundations of the Rose and Globe theaters have revealed that the open-air theater of the 1590s and later was probably a polygonal building with fourteen to twenty or twenty-four sides, multistoried, from 75 to 100 feet in diameter, with a raised, partly covered "thrust" stage that projected into a group of standing patrons, or "groundlings," and a covered gallery, seating up to 2,500 or more (very crowded) spectators.

These theaters might have been about half full on any given day, though the audiences were larger on holidays or when a play was advertised, as old and new were, through printed playbills posted around London. The metropolitan area's late-Tudor, early-Stuart population (circa 1590–1620) has been estimated at about 150,000 to 250,000. It has been supposed that in the mid-1590s there were about 15,000 spectators per week at the public theaters; thus, as many as 10 percent of the local population went to the theater regularly. Consequently, the theaters' repertories – the plays available for this experienced and frequent audience – had to change often: in the month between September 15 and October 15, 1595, for instance, the Lord Admiral's Men performed twenty-eight times in eighteen different plays.

Since natural light illuminated the amphitheaters' stages, performances began between noon and two o'clock and ran without a break for two or three hours. They often concluded with a jig, a fencing display, or some other nondramatic exhibition. Weather conditions determined the season for the amphitheaters: plays were performed every day (including Sundays, sometimes, to clerical dismay) except during Lent – the forty days before Easter – or periods of plague, or sometimes during the summer months when law courts were not in session and the most affluent members of the audience were not in London.

To a modern theatergoer, an amphitheater stage like that of the Rose or Globe would appear an unfamiliar mixture of plainness and elaborate decoration. Much of the structure was carved or painted, sometimes to imitate marble; elsewhere, as under the canopy projecting over the stage, to represent the stars and the zodiac. Appropriate painted canvas pictures (of Jerusalem, for example, if the play was set in that city) were apparently hung on the wall behind the acting area, and tragedies were accompanied by black hangings, presumably something like crepe festoons or bunting. Although these theaters did not employ what we would call scenery, early modern spectators saw numerous large props, such as the "bar" at which a prisoner stood during a trial, the "mossy bank" where lovers reclined, an arbor for amorous conversation, a chariot, gallows, tables, trees, beds, thrones, writing desks, and so forth. Audiences might learn a scene's location from a sign (reading "Athens," for example) carried across the stage (as in Bertolt Brecht's twentieth-century productions). Equally captivating (and equally irritating to the theater's enemies) were the rich costumes and personal props the actors used: the most valuable items in the surviving theatrical inventories are the swords, gowns, robes, crowns, and other items worn or carried by the performers.

Magic appealed to Shakespeare's audiences as much as it does to us today, and the theater exploited many deceptive and spectacular devices. A winch in the loft above the stage, called "the heavens," could lower and raise actors playing gods, goddesses, and other supernatural figures to and from the main acting area, just as one or more trapdoors permitted entrances and exits to and from the area, called "hell," beneath the stage. Actors wore elementary makeup such as wigs, false beards, and face paint, and they employed pig's bladders filled with animal blood to make wounds seem more real. They had rudimentary but effective ways of pretending to behead or hang a person. Supernumeraries (stagehands or actors not needed in a particular scene) could make thunder sounds (by shaking a metal sheet or rolling an iron ball down a chute) and show lightning (by blowing inflammable resin through tubes into a flame). Elaborate fireworks enhanced the effects of dragons flying through the air or imitated such celestial phenomena as comets, shooting stars, and multiple suns. Horses' hoofbeats, bells (located perhaps in the tower above the stage), trumpets and drums, clocks, cannon shots and gunshots, and the like were common sound effects. And the music of viols, cornets, oboes, and recorders was a regular feature of theatrical performances.

For two relatively brief spans, from the late 1570s to 1590 and from 1599 to 1614, the amphitheaters competed with the so-called private, or indoor, theaters, which originated as, or later represented themselves as, educational institutions training boys as singers for church services and court performances. These indoor theaters had two features that were distinct from the amphitheaters': their personnel and their playing spaces. The amphitheaters' adult companies included both adult men, who played the male roles, and boys, who played the female roles; the private, or indoor, theater companies, on the other hand, were entirely composed of boys aged about 8 to 16, who were, or could pretend to be, candidates for singers in a church or a royal boys' choir. (Until 1660, professional theatrical companies included no women.) The playing space would appear much more familiar to modern audiences than the long-vanished amphitheaters; the later indoor theaters were, in fact, the ancestors of the typical modern theater. They were enclosed spaces, usually rectangular, with the stage filling one end of the rectangle and the audience arrayed in seats or benches across (and sometimes lining) the building's longer axis. These spaces staged plays less frequently than the public theaters (perhaps only once a week) and held far fewer spectators than the amphitheaters: about 200 to 600, as opposed to 2,500 or more. Fewer patrons mean a smaller gross income, unless each pays more. Not surprisingly, then, private theaters charged higher prices than the amphitheaters, probably sixpence, as opposed to a penny for the cheapest entry.

Protected from the weather, the indoor theaters presented plays later in the day than the amphitheaters, and used artificial illumination – candles in sconces or candelabra. But candles melt, and need replacing, snuffing, and trimming, and these practical requirements may have been part of the reason the indoor theaters introduced breaks in the performance, the intermission so dear to the heart of theatergoers and to the pocketbooks of theater concessionaires ever since. Whether motivated by the need to tend to the candles or by the entrepreneurs' wishing to sell oranges and liquor, or both, the indoor theaters eventually established the modern convention of the non-continuous performance. In the early modern "private" theater, musical performances apparently filled the intermissions, which in Stuart theater jargon seem to have been called "acts."

At the end of the first decade of the seventeenth century, the distinction between public amphitheaters and private indoor companies ceased. For various cultural, political, and economic reasons, individual companies gained control of both the public, open-air theaters and the indoor ones, and companies mixing adult men and boys took over the formerly "private" theaters. Despite the death of the boys' companies and of their highly innovative theaters (for which such luminous playwrights as Ben Jonson, George Chapman, and John Marston wrote), their playing spaces and conventions had an immense impact on subsequent plays: not merely for the intervals (which stressed the artistic and architectonic importance of "acts"), but also because they introduced political and social satire as a popular dramatic ingredient, even in tragedy, and a wider range of actorly effects, encouraged by their more intimate playing spaces.

Even the briefest sketch of the Shakespearean theatrical world would be incomplete without some comment on the social and cultural dimensions of theaters and playing in the period. In an intensely hierarchical and status-conscious society, professional actors and their ventures had hardly any respectability; as we have indicated, to protect themselves against laws designed to curb vagabondage and the increase of masterless men, actors resorted to the near-fiction that they were the servants of noble masters, and wore their distinctive livery. Hence the company for which Shakespeare wrote in the 1590s called itself the Lord Chamberlain's Men and pretended that the public, money-getting performances were in fact rehearsals for private performances before that high court official. From 1598, the Privy Council had licensed theatrical companies, and after 1603, with the accession of King James I, the companies gained explicit royal protection, just as the Queen's Men had for a time under Queen Elizabeth. The Chamberlain's Men became the King's Men, and the other companies were patronized by the other members of the royal family.

These designations were legal fictions that half-concealed an important economic and social development, the evolution away from the theater's organization on the model of the guild, a self-regulating confraternity of individual artisans, into a proto-capitalist organization. Shakespeare's company became a joint-stock company, where persons who supplied capital and, in some cases, such as Shakespeare's, capital and talent, employed themselves and others in earning a return on that capital. This development meant that actors and theater companies were outside both the traditional guild structures, which required some form of civic or royal charter, and the feudal household organization of master-and-servant. This anomalous, maverick social and economic condition made theater companies practically unruly and potentially even dangerous; consequently, numerous official bodies – including the London metropolitan and ecclesiastical authorities as well as, occasionally, the royal court itself – tried, without much success, to control and even to disband them.

Public officials had good reason to want to close the theaters: they were attractive nuisances – they drew often riotous crowds, they were always noisy, and they could be politically offensive and socially insubordinate. Until the Civil War, however, anti-theatrical forces failed to shut down professional theater, for many reasons – limited surveillance and few police powers, tensions or outright hostilities among the agencies that sought to check or channel theatrical activity, and lack of clear policies for control. Another reason must have been the theaters' undeniable popularity. Curtailing any activity enjoyed by such a substantial percentage of the population was difficult, as various Roman emperors attempting to limit circuses had learned, and the Tudor-Stuart audience was not merely large, it was socially diverse and included women. The prevalence of public entertainment in this period has been underestimated. In fact, fairs, holidays, games, sporting events, the equivalent of modern parades, freak shows, and street exhibitions all abounded, but the theater was the most widely and frequently available entertainment to which people of every class had access. That fact helps account both for its quantity and for the fear and anger it aroused.

WILLIAM SHAKESPEARE OF
STRATFORD-UPON-AVON, GENTLEMAN

Many people have said that we know very little about William Shakespeare's life – pinheads and postcards are often mentioned as appropriately tiny surfaces on which to record the available information. More imaginatively and perhaps more correctly, Ralph Waldo Emerson wrote, "Shakespeare is the only biographer of Shakespeare. . . . So far from Shakespeare's being the least known, he is the one person in all modern history fully known to us."

In fact, we know more about Shakespeare's life than we do about almost any other English writer's of his era. His last will and testament (dated March 25, 1616) survives, as do numerous legal contracts and court documents involving Shakespeare as principal or witness, and parish records in Stratford and London. Shakespeare appears quite often in official records of King James's royal court, and of course Shakespeare's name appears on numerous title pages and in the written and recorded words of his literary contemporaries Robert Greene, Henry Chettle, Francis Meres, John Davies of Hereford, Ben Jonson, and many others. Indeed, if we make due allowance for the bloating of modern, run-of-the-mill bureaucratic records, more information has survived over the past four hundred years about William Shakespeare of Stratford-upon-Avon, Warwickshire, than is likely to survive in the next four hundred years about any reader of these words.

What we do not have are entire categories of information – Shakespeare's private letters or diaries, drafts and revisions of poems and plays, critical prefaces or essays, commendatory verse for other writers' works, or instructions guiding his fellow actors in their performances, for instance – that we imagine would help us understand and appreciate his surviving writings. For all we know, many such data never existed as written records. Many literary and theatrical critics, not knowing what might once have existed, more or less cheerfully accept the situation; some even make a theoretical virtue of it by claiming that such data are irrelevant to understanding and interpreting the plays and poems.

So, what do we know about William Shakespeare, the man responsible for thirty-seven or perhaps more plays, more than 150 sonnets, two lengthy narrative poems, and some shorter poems?

While many families by the name of Shakespeare (or some variant spelling) can be identified in the English Midlands as far back as the twelfth century, it seems likely that the dramatist's grandfather, Richard, moved to Snitterfield, a town not far from Stratford-upon-Avon, sometime before 1529. In Snitterfield, Richard Shakespeare leased farmland from the very wealthy Robert Arden. By 1552, Richard's son John had moved to a large house on Henley Street in Stratford-upon-Avon, the house that stands today as "The Birthplace." In Stratford, John Shakespeare traded as a glover, dealt in wool, and lent money at interest; he also served in a variety of civic posts, including "High Bailiff," the municipality's equivalent of mayor. In 1557, he married Robert Arden's youngest daughter, Mary. Mary and John had four sons – William was the oldest – and four daughters, of whom only Joan outlived her most celebrated sibling. William was baptized (an event entered in the Stratford parish church records) on April 26, 1564, and it has become customary, without any good factual support, to suppose he was born on April 23, which happens to be the feast day of Saint George, patron saint of England, and is also the date on which he died, in 1616. Shakespeare married Anne Hathaway in 1582, when he was eighteen and she was twenty-six; their first child was born five months later. It has been generally assumed that the marriage was enforced and subsequently unhappy, but these are only assumptions; it has been estimated, for instance, that up to one third of Elizabethan

brides were pregnant when they married. Anne and
William Shakespeare had three children: Susanna, who
married a prominent local physician, John Hall; and the
twins Hamnet, who died young in 1596, and Judith, who
married Thomas Quiney – apparently a rather shady individual. The name Hamnet was unusual but not unique: he
and his twin sister were named for their godparents,
Shakespeare's neighbors Hamnet and Judith Sadler. Shakespeare's father died in 1601 (the year of *Hamlet*), and Mary
Arden Shakespeare died in 1608 (the year of *Coriolanus*).
William Shakespeare's last surviving direct descendant was
his granddaughter Elizabeth Hall, who died in 1670.

Between the birth of the twins in 1585 and a clear reference to Shakespeare as a practicing London dramatist in
Robert Greene's sensationalizing, satiric pamphlet, *Greene's
Groatsworth of Wit* (1592), there is no record of where
William Shakespeare was or what he was doing. These
seven so-called lost years have been imaginatively filled by
scholars and other students of Shakespeare: some think
he traveled to Italy, or fought in the Low Countries, or
studied law or medicine, or worked as an apprentice
actor/writer, and so on to even more fanciful possibilities.
Whatever the biographical facts for those "lost" years,
Greene's nasty remarks in 1592 testify to professional envy
and to the fact that Shakespeare already had a successful career in London. Speaking to his fellow playwrights, Greene
warns both generally and specifically:

> . . . trust them [actors] not: for there is an upstart
> crow, beautified with our feathers, that with his
> tiger's heart wrapped in a player's hide supposes he is
> as well able to bombast out a blank verse as the best
> of you; and being an absolute Johannes Factotum, is
> in his own conceit the only Shake-scene in a country.

The passage mimics a line from *3 Henry VI* (hence the play
must have been performed before Greene wrote) and

seems to say that "Shake-scene" is both actor and playwright, a jack-of-all-trades. That same year, Henry Chettle protested Greene's remarks in *Kind-Heart's Dream*, and each of the next two years saw the publication of poems – *Venus and Adonis* and *The Rape of Lucrece*, respectively – publicly ascribed to (and dedicated by) Shakespeare. Early in 1595 he was named as one of the senior members of a prominent acting company, the Lord Chamberlain's Men, when they received payment for court performances during the 1594 Christmas season.

Clearly, Shakespeare had achieved both success and reputation in London. In 1596, upon Shakespeare's application, the College of Arms granted his father the now-familiar coat of arms he had taken the first steps to obtain almost twenty years before, and in 1598, John's son – now permitted to call himself "gentleman" – took a 10 percent share in the new Globe playhouse. In 1597, he bought a substantial bourgeois house, called New Place, in Stratford – the garden remains, but Shakespeare's house, several times rebuilt, was torn down in 1759 – and over the next few years Shakespeare spent large sums buying land and making other investments in the town and its environs. Though he worked in London, his family remained in Stratford, and he seems always to have considered Stratford the home he would eventually return to. Something approaching a disinterested appreciation of Shakespeare's popular and professional status appears in Francis Meres's *Palladis Tamia* (1598), a not especially imaginative and perhaps therefore persuasive record of literary reputations. Reviewing contemporary English writers, Meres lists the titles of many of Shakespeare's plays, including one not now known, *Love's Labor's Won*, and praises his "mellifluous & hony-tongued" "sugred Sonnets," which were then circulating in manuscript (they were first collected in 1609). Meres describes Shakespeare as "one of the best" English playwrights of both comedy and tragedy. In *Remains . . . Concerning Britain* (1605),

William Camden – a more authoritative source than the imitative Meres – calls Shakespeare one of the "most pregnant witts of these our times" and joins him with such writers as Chapman, Daniel, Jonson, Marston, and Spenser. During the first decades of the seventeenth century, publishers began to attribute numerous play quartos, including some non-Shakespearean ones, to Shakespeare, either by name or initials, and we may assume that they deemed Shakespeare's name and supposed authorship, true or false, commercially attractive.

For the next ten years or so, various records show Shakespeare's dual career as playwright and man of the theater in London, and as an important local figure in Stratford. In 1608-9 his acting company – designated the "King's Men" soon after King James had succeeded Queen Elizabeth in 1603 – rented, refurbished, and opened a small interior playing space, the Blackfriars theater, in London, and Shakespeare was once again listed as a substantial sharer in the group of proprietors of the playhouse. By May 11, 1612, however, he describes himself as a Stratford resident in a London lawsuit – an indication that he had withdrawn from day-to-day professional activity and returned to the town where he had always had his main financial interests. When Shakespeare bought a substantial residential building in London, the Blackfriars Gatehouse, close to the theater of the same name, on March 10, 1613, he is recorded as William Shakespeare "of Stratford upon Avon in the county of Warwick, gentleman," and he named several London residents as the building's trustees. Still, he continued to participate in theatrical activity: when the new Earl of Rutland needed an allegorical design to bear as a shield, or *impresa*, at the celebration of King James's Accession Day, March 24, 1613, the earl's accountant recorded a payment of 44 shillings to Shakespeare for the device with its motto.

For the last few years of his life, Shakespeare evidently

concentrated his activities in the town of his birth. Most of the final records concern business transactions in Stratford, ending with the notation of his death on April 23, 1616, and burial in Holy Trinity Church, Stratford-upon-Avon.

THE QUESTION OF AUTHORSHIP

The history of ascribing Shakespeare's plays (the poems do not come up so often) to someone else began, as it continues, peculiarly. The earliest published claim that someone else wrote Shakespeare's plays appeared in an 1856 article by Delia Bacon in the American journal *Putnam's Monthly* – although an Englishman, Thomas Wilmot, had shared his doubts in private (even secretive) conversations with friends near the end of the eighteenth century. Bacon's was a sad personal history that ended in madness and poverty, but the year after her article, she published, with great difficulty and the bemused assistance of Nathaniel Hawthorne (then United States Consul in Liverpool, England), her *Philosophy of the Plays of Shakspere Unfolded*. This huge, ornately written, confusing farrago is almost unreadable; sometimes its intents, to say nothing of its arguments, disappear entirely beneath near-raving, ecstatic writing. Tumbled in with much supposed "philosophy" appear the claims that Francis Bacon (from whom Delia Bacon eventually claimed descent), Walter Ralegh, and several other contemporaries of Shakespeare's had written the plays. The book had little impact except as a ridiculed curiosity.

Once proposed, however, the issue gained momentum among people whose conviction was the greater in proportion to their ignorance of sixteenth- and seventeenth-century English literature, history, and society. Another American amateur, Catherine P. Ashmead Windle, made the next influential contribution to the cause when she published *Report to the British Museum* (1882), wherein she promised to open "the Cipher of Francis Bacon," though what she mostly offers, in the words of S. Schoenbaum, is "demented allegorizing." An entire new cottage industry grew from Windle's suggestion that the texts contain hidden, cryptographically discoverable ciphers – "clues" – to their authorship; and today there are not only books devoted to the putative ciphers, but also pamphlets, journals, and newsletters.

Although Baconians have led the pack of those seeking a substitute Shakespeare, in *"Shakespeare" Identified* (1920), J. Thomas Looney became the first published "Oxfordian" when he proposed Edward de Vere, seventeenth earl of Oxford, as the secret author of Shakespeare's plays. Also for Oxford and his "authorship" there are today dedicated societies, articles, journals, and books. Less popular candidates – Queen Elizabeth and Christopher Marlowe among them – have had adherents, but the movement seems to have divided into two main contending factions, Baconian and Oxfordian. (For further details on all the candidates for "Shakespeare," see S. Schoenbaum, *Shakespeare's Lives,* 2nd ed., 1991.)

The Baconians, the Oxfordians, and supporters of other candidates have one trait in common – they are snobs. Every pro-Bacon or pro-Oxford tract sooner or later claims that the historical William Shakespeare of Stratford-upon-Avon could not have written the plays because he could not have had the training, the university education, the experience, and indeed the imagination or background their author supposedly possessed. Only a learned genius like Bacon or an aristocrat like Oxford could have written such fine plays. (As it happens, lucky male children of the middle class had access to better education than most aristocrats in Elizabethan England – and Oxford was not particularly well educated.) Shakespeare received in the Stratford grammar school a formal education that would daunt many college graduates today; and popular rival playwrights such as the very learned Ben Jonson and George Chapman, both of whom also lacked university training, achieved great artistic success, without being taken as Bacon or Oxford.

Besides snobbery, one other quality characterizes the authorship controversy: lack of evidence. A great deal of testimony from Shakespeare's time shows that Shakespeare wrote Shakespeare's plays and that his contemporaries recognized them as distinctive and distinctly superior. (Some of that contemporary evidence is collected in E. K. Chambers, *William Shakespeare: A Study of Facts and Problems,* 2 vols., 1930.) Since that testimony comes from Shakespeare's enemies and theatrical competitors as well as from his co-workers and from the Elizabethan equivalent of literary journalists, it seems unlikely that, if any of these sources had known he was a fraud, they would have failed to record that fact.

Books About Shakespeare's Theater

Useful scholarly studies of theatrical life in Shakespeare's day include: G. E. Bentley, *The Jacobean and Caroline Stage,* 7 vols. (1941-68), and the same author's *The Professions of Dramatist and Player in Shakespeare's Time, 1590-1642* (1986); E. K. Chambers, *The Elizabethan Stage,* 4 vols. (1923); R. A. Foakes, *Illustrations of the English Stage, 1580-1642* (1985); Andrew Gurr, *The Shakespearean Stage,* 3rd ed. (1992), and the same author's *Play-going in Shakespeare's London,* 2nd ed. (1996); Edwin Nungezer, *A Dictionary of Actors* (1929); Carol Chillington Rutter, ed., *Documents of the Rose Playhouse* (1984).

Books About Shakespeare's Life

The following books provide scholarly, documented accounts of Shakespeare's life: G. E. Bentley, *Shakespeare: A Biographical Handbook* (1961); E. K. Chambers, *William Shakespeare: A Study of Facts and Problems,* 2 vols. (1930); S. Schoenbaum, *William Shakespeare: A Compact*

Documentary Life (1977); and *Shakespeare's Lives,* 2nd ed. (1991), by the same author. Many scholarly editions of Shakespeare's complete works print brief compilations of essential dates and events. References to Shakespeare's works up to 1700 are collected in C. M. Ingleby et al., *The Shakespeare Allusion-Book,* rev. ed., 2 vols. (1932).

The Texts of Shakespeare

As FAR AS WE KNOW, only one manuscript conceivably in Shakespeare's own hand may (and even this is much disputed) exist: a few pages of a play called *Sir Thomas More*, which apparently was never performed. What we do have, as later readers, performers, scholars, students, are printed texts. The earliest of these survive in two forms: quartos and folios. Quartos (from the Latin for "four") are small books, printed on sheets of paper that were then folded in fours, to make eight double-sided pages. When these were bound together, the result was a squarish, eminently portable volume that sold for the relatively small sum of sixpence (translating in modern terms to about $5.00). In folios, on the other hand, the sheets are folded only once, in half, producing large, impressive volumes taller than they are wide. This was the format for important works of philosophy, science, theology, and literature (the major precedent for a folio Shakespeare was Ben Jonson's *Works*, 1616). The decision to print the works of a popular playwright in folio is an indication of how far up on the social scale the theatrical profession had come during Shakespeare's lifetime. The Shakespeare folio was an expensive book, selling for between fifteen and eighteen shillings, depending on the binding (in modern terms, from about $150 to $180). Twenty Shakespeare plays of the thirty-seven that survive first appeared in quarto, seventeen of which appeared during Shakespeare's lifetime; the rest of the plays are found only in folio.

The First Folio was published in 1623, seven years after Shakespeare's death, and was authorized by his fellow actors, the co-owners of the King's Men. This publication was certainly a mark of the company's enormous respect for Shakespeare; but it was also a way of turning the old plays, most of which were no longer current in the playhouse, into ready money (the folio includes only Shakespeare's plays, not his sonnets or other nondramatic verse). Whatever the motives behind the publication of the folio, the texts it preserves constitute the basis for almost all later editions of the playwright's works. The texts, however, differ from those of the earlier quartos, sometimes in minor respects but often significantly – most strikingly in the two texts of *King Lear,* but also in important ways in *Hamlet, Othello,* and *Troilus and Cressida.* (The variants are recorded in the textual notes to each play in the new Pelican series.) The differences in these texts represent, in a sense, the essence of theater: the texts of plays were initially not intended for publication. They were scripts, designed for the actors to perform – the principal life of the play at this period was in performance. And it follows that in Shakespeare's theater the playwright typically had no say either in how his play was performed or in the disposition of his text – he was an employee of the company. The authoritative figures in the theatrical enterprise were the shareholders in the company, who were for the most part the major actors. They decided what plays were to be done; they hired the playwright and often gave him an outline of the play they wanted him to write. Often, too, the play was a collaboration: the company would retain a group of writers, and parcel out the scenes among them. The resulting script was then the property of the company, and the actors would revise it as they saw fit during the course of putting it on stage. The resulting text belonged to the company. The playwright had no rights in it once he had been paid. (This system survives largely intact in the movie industry, and most of the playwrights of Shakespeare's time were as anonymous as most screenwriters are today.) The script could also, of course, continue to change as the tastes of audiences and the requirements of the actors changed. Many – perhaps most – plays were revised when they were reintroduced after any substantial absence from the repertory, or when they were performed by a company different from the one that originally commissioned the play.

Shakespeare was an exceptional figure in this world because he was not only a shareholder and actor in his company, but also its leading playwright – he was literally his own boss. He had, moreover, little interest in the publication of his plays, and even those that appeared during his lifetime with the authorization of the company show no signs of any editorial concern on the part of the author. Theater was, for Shakespeare, a fluid and supremely responsive medium – the very opposite of the great classic canonical text that has embodied his works since 1623.

The very fluidity of the original texts, however, has meant that Shakespeare has always had to be edited. Here is an example of how problematic the editorial project inevitably is, a passage from the most famous speech in *Romeo and Juliet,* Juliet's balcony soliloquy beginning "O Romeo, Romeo, wherefore art thou Romeo?" Since the eighteenth century, the standard modern text has read,

> What's Montague? It is nor hand, nor foot,
> Nor arm, nor face, nor any other part
> Belonging to a man. O be some other name!
> What's in a name? That which we call a rose
> By any other name would smell as sweet.
>
> (II.2.40–44)

Editors have three early texts of this play to work from, two quarto texts and the folio. Here is how the First Quarto (1597) reads:

> Whats *Mountague*? It is nor band nor foote,
> Nor arme, nor face, nor any other part.
> Whats in a name? That which we call a Rofe,
> By any other name would fmell as fweet:

Here is the Second Quarto (1599):

> Whats *Mountague*? it is nor hand nor foote,
> Nor arme nor face, ô be fome other name
> Belonging to a man.
> Whats in a name that which we call a rofe,
> By any other word would fmell as fweete,

And here is the First Folio (1623):

> What's *Mountague*? it is nor hand nor foote,
> Nor arme, nor face, O be fome other name
> Belonging to a man.
> What? in a names that which we call a Rofe,
> By any other word would fmell as fweete,

There is in fact no early text that reads as our modern text does — and this is the most famous speech in the play. Instead, we have three quite different texts, all of which are clearly some version of the same speech, but none of which seems to us a final or satisfactory version. The transcendently beautiful passage in modern editions is an editorial invention: editors have succeeded in conflating and revising the three versions into something we recognize as great poetry. Is this what Shakespeare "really" wrote? Who can say? What we can say is that Shakespeare always had performance, not a book, in mind.

Books About the Shakespeare Texts

The standard study of the printing history of the First Folio is W. W. Greg, *The Shakespeare First Folio* (1955). J. K. Walton, *The Quarto Copy for the First Folio of Shakespeare*

(1971), is a useful survey of the relation of the quartos to the folio. The second edition of Charlton Hinman's *Norton Facsimile* of the First Folio (1996), with a new introduction by Peter Blayney, is indispensable. Stanley Wells, Gary Taylor, John Jowett, and William Montgomery, *William Shakespeare: A Textual Companion,* keyed to the Oxford text, gives a comprehensive survey of the editorial situation for all the plays and poems.

THE GENERAL EDITORS

Introduction

THE OPENING ACT of *As You Like It* (c. 1599-1600) might lead us to expect a swift, unhappy ending. We begin in a corrupt and suspicious court, a world in which an older brother not only gets the land and the title (as was usually the case under primogeniture), but schemes to deny his younger brother an appropriate education and class standing. Compared to the lovable Orlando, the older Oliver is "altogether misprised" (I.1.159); as a consequence, he is willing to condone fratricide simply because "my soul, yet I know not why, hates nothing more than he" (154-55). Deadly sibling rivalry occupies many of Shakespeare's histories and tragedies; it also stakes out the moral terrain of this comedy. Two sets of brothers – not only Oliver and Orlando, but also Dukes Senior and Frederick – divide the world between them, the evil brothers presiding over the court, and the benevolent, wronged, banished brothers creating an alternative, "green" world in the Forest of Arden.

Shakespeare's plays often begin off center, not with the main protagonists, but with other characters who observe and comment on them. This play is no exception. But while it takes a while for the focus to shift to Rosalind, one of Shakespeare's liveliest heroines, and the comic business of coupling, this dark opening also reveals a great deal about the concerns of the play, about what will be accomplished and resolved in its course. Four pairs of "country copulatives" will take their vows, and Hymen will people every town, but brothers will also be reconciled, and legitimacy and property restored; the virtuous will be rewarded with property, power, and love; a younger brother will succeed to his father's estate; the evil will miraculously convert; and, despite disguise and dislocation, each lover will meet his or her social match. In short, order will be renewed and restored through a temporary detour into disorder; attachment will be achieved through banishment.

The setting in which such things are possible is both England – there is a Forest of Arden in Warwickshire, and Shakespeare's mother's name was Mary Arden – and France – since some of the characters' names suggest a French setting, as does the reference to "Robin Hood of England" (I.1.111). As both "here" and "there" the setting seems to be both nowhere and everywhere. This is a magical place in which one can imagine alternatives, play roles, explore possibilities. As Touchstone remarks, "Your If is the only peacemaker. Much virtue in If" (V.4.101). In Arden, Rosalind can invite Orlando – and herself – to imagine what life would be like "and I were your very very Rosalind" (IV.1.65-66). Her complex series of riddles, by which she vows to resolve all conflicts by being herself, revolves around "if": "if I can"; "if I could"; "if ever I marry woman"; "if ever I satisfied man"; "if what pleases you contents you" (V.2.106-11).

In Arden, even the villains can miraculously shed their former selves. As Oliver explains to Celia, " 'Twas I. But 'tis not I" (IV.3.134). Like Eden, Arden is not wholly safe. It is cold there, and people are hungry and must hunt for food. Lions and snakes threaten sudden death. Nor is Arden safe from invasion. Returning us to Duke Frederick's court, Act III, scene 1 reminds us that it continues to exist and that it threatens to impinge on the characters in Arden. While the characters in the forest must feed themselves, for the most part they have the luxury of leisure. Even Silvius and Phebe seem to have little to do. Corin alone is a "true laborer; I earn that I eat, get that I wear, . . . and the greatest of my pride is to see my ewes graze and my lambs suck" (III.2.70-74). Almost everyone else finds plenty of time to sing, versify, philosophize, or fall in love.

This pastoral place is not an alternative to civilization,

"nature" as opposed to "culture." Instead, it is a place where the denizens of the court go to renew themselves, and where they literally leave their mark. The landscape is articulate, legible, literary. There are "tongues in trees, books in the running brooks, / Sermons in stones" (II.1.16-17). Having first determined to read this book of nature – "these trees shall be my books" (III.2.5) – Orlando then decides to rewrite it instead: "Tongues I'll hang on every tree" (124). Others object to Orlando's crude literalism (and vandalism): Jaques pleads with him to "mar no more trees with writing love songs in their barks" (254-55); Rosalind chides, "There is a man haunts the forest that abuses our young plants with carving 'Rosalind' on their barks" (348-50). Orlando's graffiti on the trees hardly distinguish him among pastoral lovers. In Sir Philip Sidney's *Arcadia* (1590), characters frequently write on natural objects; in Lady Mary Wroth's *Urania* (1621), Pamphilia busily carves whole sonnets in the bark of trees. Shakespeare's parody of the tradition reminds us how very conventional Orlando's conduct is. He has learned that this is how lovers should act, not from trees but from poems and romances. Similarly, Silvius and Phebe are shepherds who seem to have taken a college survey course in early British literature. Their ideas about love are, as Juliet says of Romeo's first kiss, "by th' book." While Rosalind and Orlando speak to each other in prose, Phebe and Silvius speak in verse (in III.5), reminding us that they are in a literary world that shapes rather than reflects experience. By challenging these conventions and their relation in experience, Rosalind strives to forge a love that can survive outside the covers of a book and outside Arden, every rainy day as well as "ever and a day." *As You Like It* is not just about love, then, but about how people write about love, how those writings shape expectation, and what happens when our ideals are hung on trees for all to see and scrutinize.

In her game with Orlando, Rosalind attempts both to

educate him in the conventions of love and to put pressure on those conventions: "Men have died from time to time, and worms have eaten them, but not for love" (IV.1.98-100). One reason to test Orlando in this way is that, as Touchstone points out, both lovers and poets are given to feigning (III.3.17-20). Phebe, Silvius, and Rosalind all hold forth on the literary lover's attributes. But once one learns the part, how is the beloved to tell whether one's love is true or simply well played? How can one separate content and form, truth and fiction, feeling and script? Since, in the course of the play, both Orlando and Rosalind plumb their "true" feelings by means of performances, the distinction between the true and the feigned never emerges clearly.

Here we see Shakespeare's relation to one of his sources, Thomas Lodge's prose romance *Rosalynde, Euphues' Golden Legacie* (1590). With his usual free hand, Shakespeare borrows liberally from Lodge's plot and characters. Shakespeare expands the part of Rosalind, trims the part of Orlando (who in the source writes lots of poetry but also spends a great deal of time fighting, rescuing, and killing), expands the part of the banished duke, and makes the two dukes brothers (and thus Celia and Rosalind cousins). He excises a bloody battle between the two dukes that ends in the usurper's death, replacing it with Duke Frederick's conversion and retirement. He invents Jaques, Touchstone, and Audrey. Through Touchstone, Shakespeare parodies the excessive and bombastic style that characterizes his source, as well as John Lyly's *Euphues, the Anatomy of Wit* (1579). Thus Shakespeare borrows the pleasures and possibilities of the pastoral retreat, but also probes and satirizes them. Perhaps this helps to explain why Rosalind is so hard on Phebe, a literary character who wanders out into life, revealing how limited are the literary conventions of unrequited love and maidenly disdain. Yet Rosalind's contempt for Phebe is also somewhat snobby and cruel. Surely, Rosalind would not greet

Silvius's courtship with a "coming on disposition." Why can Rosalind test her suitor while Phebe is sternly advised to drop to her knees and "thank heaven, fasting, for a good man's love" (III.5.58); "Sell when you can, you are not for all markets" (60)? To find this funny, we must accept that Phebe deserves less than Rosalind, perhaps because she is a shepherdess rather than a duke's daughter, and because she is less pretty. We must accept that her longing is foolish and her delay is presumptuous.

Arden is not only a literary world, but a musical one. *As You Like It* contains more songs than any other Shakespeare play. The most famous of these is "It was a lover and his lass," sung by two pages in V.3. The song was arranged as a two-part madrigal by Thomas Morley and published in his *First Book of Ayres* (1600); Morley's may have been the music used in the first performances of the play. Because the folio does not clearly indicate who was to sing many of the other songs, it is hard to know for sure. Except for the songs sung by Hymen at the end of the play, they are often attributed to Amiens, assumed to be an adult male singer, who has little else to do in the play save sing. These songs contribute to the "hey nonny nonny" (or "hey nonino"), "merry old England" feel of the play. More substantially, they participate in the characters' incessant reflections on what love is, how one can recognize it, and how we can put this intense and overwhelming experience into words. "Hey ding a ding, ding" sums up the elation of love quite nicely.

Rosalind and Orlando escape the gloom, confinement, and danger of the court not only by departing for the forest, albeit under duress, but by growing up. For Rosalind and Orlando, Celia and Oliver, this means moving from the family into which one is born to the family one starts and presides over, or, as Rosalind frankly puts it, from one's father to one's child's father (I.3.10-11). In Duke Frederick's court, the young people all seem to have the wrong fathers: Duke Frederick tells Orlando, "I

would thou hadst been son to some man else" (I.2.211);
his reason for banishing Rosalind is that she is her "father's daughter, there's enough" (I.3.56); Celia is so em-
barrassed by her own father that she offers to trade with
Rosalind (89). In the Forest of Arden, in contrast, Duke
Senior reassures Orlando, "I am the duke / That loved
your father" (II.7.194-95). Outside the orbit of Duke
Frederick, Rosalind and Orlando both have the "right" fathers, yet they are also ceasing to define themselves in
terms of their fathers. Rosalind speedily transacts the shift
from her father to her husband, a transfer that in tragedy
is vexed or doomed. In different ways, Ophelia in *Hamlet*,
Cordelia in *King Lear*, and Desdemona in *Othello* are all
destroyed in the process of negotiating conflicting loves
and loyalties, and becoming wives as well as daughters.
For Rosalind, this is the work of an instant: "But what
talk we of fathers when there is such a man as Orlando?"
(III.4.35-36). When Rosalind encounters her father in
the forest, she does not identify herself, in part because to
do so would be to place herself under his protection, and
thus to limit her independence.

While the journey to the forest enables a separation
from fathers, even for Rosalind, the journey also, more
gradually, effects a separation between Celia and Rosalind. At court, their "loves / Are dearer than the natural
bond of sisters" (I.2.262-63); "never two ladies loved as
they do" (I.1.106-7). Of the two women, Celia is the one
who articulates this intimacy, insisting to her father that
she and Rosalind are "coupled and inseparable" (I.3.74),
and reminding Rosalind that "thou and I am one" (95).
Duke Frederick attempts to drive a wedge between the
cousins, urging Celia to view Rosalind as her rival (78ff).
But what ultimately divides them is love and marriage. As
Rosalind/Ganymede becomes involved with Orlando,
Celia, who initially proposed that they run away together,
and insisted on the depth and significance of their attach-

ment, finds herself on the margins of the action, often with little to say. At first, she finds her tongue to ridicule Orlando's poetry and Rosalind's besotted state. Then her anger at Rosalind becomes more pointed; her sense that Rosalind not only abandons her but maligns women is not just sour grapes, as some critics have argued, but has some foundation. In Act IV.1 Celia has no lines at all during an extended exchange between Rosalind and Orlando. At the close of the scene, she announces, foolishly, "I'll sleep" (IV.1.205). What else is left for her to do? She needs to fall in love with Oliver, if only to move back toward the center of action.

Critics once assumed that the attachment between Rosalind and Celia was a stage that they would have to outgrow; by this logic, Celia and Rosalind move through their identification with each other, to the apparently same-sex friendship between Ganymede and Orlando, to marriage. In this view, maturity in comedies is manifested in marriage. Thus it is, at best, immature for women to fall in love with women, or for men to love men. By this logic, one critic referred to Phebe's "aberrant" or "mistaken" attraction to Rosalind. More recently, critics have questioned the assumption that same-sex attachment is a stage of arrested development, something from which one recovers. Once one surrenders that assumption, then it is possible to argue that comedies such as *As You Like It* depict the strained process by which both prospective spouses repudiate homoerotic attachments in the service of the marital bond. These comedies enact a fantasy of how marriage works to create and support an erotic and procreative bond between a man and a woman, distinguishing it from and privileging it over other relations. The threat to marriage is not only Rosalind's attachment to Celia, but Orlando's attachment to Ganymede. Subordinating these earlier attachments to the marital bond is not easy. The young lovers do not simply grow into marriage. Instead, the play shows us that the process by which they shift their allegiances requires time, relocation, magic, ingenuity, and disguise.

Why, precisely, must Rosalind disguise herself? At first, she assumes the disguise for protection. Since "Beauty provoketh thieves sooner than gold" (I.3.108), the young women must protect themselves from rape and assault by concealing their beauty. Each chooses a disguise that obscures her high social status. Celia also determines to darken her complexion: "I'll . . . with a kind of umber smirch my face; / The like do you" (I.3.109–11). Darkening her face will make her less recognizable; it also marks her as a working woman, exposed to the sun, and as less desirable. While Celia does not seem to wear what we would identify as "blackface," she does propose that she and Rosalind darken their faces in a way that, while not quite a matter of racial impersonation, draws on standards of beauty inflected by race as well as class. Although the association of skin color with racial difference was not clearly established at this time, the association of very pale skin with beauty or "fairness" draws on and feeds into a history of assigning moral and aesthetic value to color, which corresponds to a history of racism. Instead of lowering herself on a scale of status and racialized beauty, however, Rosalind chooses to raise herself in the hierarchy of gender, dressing herself as a man. In addition, Rosalind proposes that she should be called "Ganymede," Jove's page and cupbearer, frequently understood as his lover.

The disguises, particularly Rosalind's, enable much more than a safe journey to and stay in Arden. For if that were the sole purpose of the disguise, why would Rosalind neglect to identify herself to her father or to Orlando? From the start, Rosalind especially seems to relish the prospect of playing the man. The disguises provide the "sports" the young women earlier sought to divert themselves (I.2.24). Disguise also seems to afford Rosalind a wider range of movement and capacity for action, although the oft-repeated claim that Rosalind cannot buy the cottage unless she is disguised as a man seems wrong. Within the world of the play, Rosalind employs Corin to buy the cottage, pasture, and flock (apparently out from under Silvius) on her behalf. In sixteenth- and seventeenth-century England, unmarried women like Rosalind, especially those who paid in cash, could buy and sell property. It was married women, not single or widowed ones, who were limited in their ability to make contracts and transact business deals.

Rosalind's disguise seems to enhance her confidence while Celia's disguise reduces her to "the weaker vessel" (II.4.6). Yet, even though Rosalind's disguise serves her courtship, there remains a tension between the Rosalind who loves Orlando and the Rosalind who relishes her disguise. Rosalind first responds to Orlando's arrival in Arden as a problem because of her disguise: "what shall I do with my doublet and hose?" (III.2.214-15); "But doth he know that I am in this forest, and in man's apparel?" (III.2.224-25). Rosalind does not, however, solve the problem by removing her disguise and revealing herself to Orlando. Why not? The disguise enables a delay between loving at first sight and plighting one's troth. By stalling, Rosalind creates a stage between leaving her father's household and entering her husband's, between her father's "giving her away" in marriage and her husband's taking her. Dressed as Ganymede, she establishes her own household and discovers or invents her own identity before she submits herself to Orlando in marriage. Whereas Shakespeare's tragedies often explore the difficulties fathers experience in surrendering their daughters to marriage, and the "divided duty" daughters experience, torn between fathers and husbands, *As You Like It* allows Ganymede and Orlando to get to know each other man to man. In the emotional and mental space between her roles as daughter and as wife, Rosalind explores the possibility of friendship, a relationship that not only does not require her subordination, but, indeed, gives her the upper hand over Orlando. Her time as Ganymede is limited, but it eases the transfer.

It also complicates the outcome. Ultimately, Rosalind surrenders her disguise and submits herself to father, husband, and a social order she has worked to revitalize and restore, rather than overturn. Yet the conclusion of the story cannot wholly forget the middle, nor can marriage utterly banish the homoerotic attachment that precedes and enables it. Does Ganymede look like a woman or a man? If Ganymede is, as Oliver has heard, "Of female favor, and bestows himself / Like a ripe sister" (IV.3.85-86), then the scenes between Ganymede and Orlando may reassure audiences with at least the appearance of heteroeroticism. But if that is the case, then the homoeroticism of Phebe's attraction to Ganymede is emphasized. Phebe is drawn to a man who looks like a woman. To a certain extent, Phebe's love for Ganymede, like Titania's love for Bottom in *A Midsummer Night's Dream,* works to humble and chasten her. "You to his love must accord, / Or have a woman to your lord" (V.4.131-32). Since the second option is presented as ridiculous and unacceptable, Phebe must take Silvius. This is explicitly presented as submitting herself to the inevitable, an extreme form of "settling." If Phebe is somehow disciplined by finding that she has fallen in love with another woman, how is Orlando to feel about the fact that he has fallen in love with Ganymede, whom he understands to be a boy? His attachment to Rosalind has deepened and grown as a relationship between a man and a boy. But, as the epilogue reminds us, when it comes down to stripping away the costume and performance of gender, both Phebe and Orlando "really" wind up with boys. Critics have long argued that the boy actor was a convention that audiences took for granted. However, this play offers no easy way out of the conundrum of same-sex attraction. If we assume that the audience perceived Ganymede as feminine, then Phebe falls for a distinctly feminine boy. If we assume that Ganymede is a convincing boy, then Phebe is back within the pale of heteroeroticism, but Orlando is caught in a mock marriage to a boy.

Still, the epilogue insists, Rosalind is neither a boy actor nor the "woman's part" he plays, neither a convincing Ganymede nor a convincing Rosalind but both. While there is a tension between boy actor and female role, between the "I" who says "If I were a woman" and the "I" who says "I make curtsy," there is also an overlap. On the one hand, this play reinforces gender norms and the assumption that certain behaviors go with certain body parts. Rosalind is "really" a woman, and, while her disguise alters her appearance, she does not "have a doublet and hose in [her] disposition" (III.2.191-92). When she is away from Orlando and in Celia's company, she reveals herself, despite her disguise, as bound by conventional femininity: she is impetuous and lovesick; whatever she thinks she must speak (244-45); she is prone to tears, even when Celia reminds her that they "do not become a man" (III.4.3); she faints at the sight of blood. Such lines reinforce the assumption that women are naturally inclined to such behavior; that gender distinctions are matters of birth and body, not education and expectation. All of this is, of course, the performance of a boy actor skilled at playing women convincingly – that is, in accord with expectations and prescriptions regarding how women should act. Rosalind sometimes discloses the femininity beneath her disguise, despite the fact that this femininity is itself a performance; at other times she rehearses conventions about women for Orlando's benefit, thereby reinforcing the appearance that she, too, is a man. She presents women as loquacious, jealous, fickle, emotionally volatile, sexually wayward. Indeed, she rehearses all of the complaints about women so tirelessly catalogued in the period. As Celia complains, "You have simply misused our sex in your love prate. We must have your doublet and hose plucked over your head, and show the world what the bird hath done to her own nest" (IV.1.188-91). Rosalind also depicts manhood as a performance, not only for her but for all "men": "We'll have a swashing and a martial outside, / As many other mannish cowards have / That do outface it with their semblances" (I.3.118-20). Perhaps this anxious awareness that the men who play men in daily life are performing as much as are the boys who play women on the stage inspires the relentless reinforcing of distinctions between men and women, masculinity and femininity, distinctions that exist largely in their reenactments.

When Rosalind sheds her disguise, she seems to split into two. Hymen absorbs Rosalind's function as the organizer and choreographer of the conclusion, while Rosalind steps into a smaller, more familiar role as bride. As Ganymede, s/he has played the role of stage manager usually reserved for men: Hamlet, Iago, the duke in *Measure for Measure*, and Prospero, for instance. Rosalind once more, she surrenders much of the mastery and independence that she had achieved through her disguise. She also achieves marriage, which, in this period, is generally the happy ending for women, their comic destiny. Hers is a marriage that seems more grounded in intimacy than the others, more likely to survive outside Arden. And it is, after all, the goal she seems to have pursued, the motive for much of her conduct.

The play ends, famously, with four sets of couples: Rosalind and Orlando; Celia and Oliver; Audrey and Touchstone; Phebe and Silvius. The last two couples have moved from triangles to duos by eliminating rivals; Touchstone beats out William, and Silvius steps in for Ganymede when "he" is revealed to be a "she." The play has prepared us to evaluate these couplings differently, and to view them as commenting on one another. In their hasty love match, Oliver and Celia dismiss all that Rosalind would say matters most. Phebe is tricked into her match with Silvius, and how happy she will be with this bargain is anybody's guess. Touchstone enacts the least sentimental attitude toward marriage, strategizing to avoid being "well married" because "it will be a good excuse for me hereafter to leave my wife" (III.3.85-86). His attitude toward his wife is unsentimental too: he calls her "an ill-favored thing, sir, but mine own" (V.4.57-58); when he instructs Audrey, "bear your body more seeming" (68-69), one has to wonder how she usually comports herself! While Touchstone, on the one hand, assumes that his happy ending may not be ever after, and Rosalind, on the other hand, has struggled to ensure and inoculate her love as much as is possible, the other two couples remain open to question.

Marriage offers a different kind of ending, as well as a different kind of beginning, for each of these couples. For all the variety of these unions, however, an underlying order grounds the festivity. Anyone can marry, from a clown to a duke's daughter, but despite disguise and disruption, each person miraculously ends up in a heterosexual union with someone of the same social standing. Options and identities are only temporarily fluid here.

Jaques's famous "All the world's a stage" set piece (II.7) puts all of the lovers' plots into perspective. Obviously, so conventional a speech rehearses an ideal prescription for the seven parts a man might play; it does not describe how lives really unfolded. It does, however, reveal cultural expectations. In its generic focus on man, the speech fails to account for the rather different stages of a woman's life, which might be expected to build toward marriage and motherhood (despite the fact that many women never married). Of the seven ages through which a man moves, only one bears on what happens in Arden: "And then the lover, / Sighing like furnace, with a woeful ballad / Made to his mistress' eyebrow" (II.7.146-48). Jaques depicts love as a youthful excess, something men grow out of on their way to maturity, which is figured not as the personal fulfillment of marriage and parenthood, but as the competence and authority earned through work as a soldier, and then a judge. This climax of a man's life is then followed by the decline into incompetence and the return to dependency. In the play, Adam might be seen as representing these final stages, in which debility reminds men not only that they are mortal, but that their virility is ephemeral. Yet, as Adam shows in his moral superiority to Oliver and Duke Frederick, his remarkable loyalty to Orlando, and his ability to endure suffering, moral fortitude can grow even as physical strength diminishes; a physical and social dependent can also be an ethical guide.

Jaques and Adam help us to put the conclusion into perspective in other ways as well. Standing outside the festive ending and refusing to join in the dance, Jaques reminds the cast and the audience that even this capacious and generous conclusion cannot include everyone. Adam reminds us that while marriage leads to births, death shadows even the happiest of lives. According to a popular story, one of Shakespeare's relatives remembered him as an actor in the part of an old man carried on another character's back. Although this story is probably apocryphal, it grew and gained currency, fueling a myth that Shakespeare was the first actor to play Adam. Whatever the truth was, the myth helps to direct our attention to this wonderful character. While a comic ending cannot include everyone, Renaissance households included many more people than we might at first expect. Surely Adam is more closely bound to Orlando than is Oliver; Celia is more bound to Rosalind than to her own father. Jaques, however much of a loner he is, attaches himself to Duke Senior, and, when Duke Frederick refuses to return to the court, announces his intention to "hear and learn" from Frederick, the recent convert. If Jaques is the play's misanthrope, he is a surprisingly sociable one. For all of its interest in marriages, the play locates the couple in a web of social relations between brothers, cousins, masters and servants, dukes and courtiers, converts and their students.

FRANCES E. DOLAN
Miami University, Ohio

Note on the Text

THE FIRST PRINTING of *As You Like It* was in the folio of 1623 (referred to below as F). Therefore, it is one of those plays that might not have survived if this folio, often referred to as the First Folio or first edition of Shakespeare's collected works, had not been printed. As is so often the case, it is difficult to determine the kind of manuscript from which the folio text was set, since no such manuscript survives. Perhaps the compositors relied on a promptbook or a transcript either of the promptbook or of the author's "foul papers." On August 4, 1600, the Lord Chamberlain's Men, the company in which Shakespeare was a shareholder, entered "As you like yt, a booke" in the Stationers' Register as one of four plays "to be staied" – that is, withheld from publication. This indicates that the play was in production at that time, even if it was not then printed.

The folio text of the play is generally considered reliable. Like most editions, this one regularizes the spelling of names, modernizes and standardizes spelling and punctuation, corrects obvious typographical errors, relineates the text – presenting some passages set as verse in the folio as prose, and provides act and scene divisions to aid study and discussion. It also adds some new stage directions or clarifications of existing stage directions, signaling these with brackets. In the speech prefixes and stage directions, the folio's references to Clowne have been changed to Touchstone throughout; Duke Frederick has been substituted for Duke; Oliver in III.3 has been specified as Sir Oliver Martext; and the Second Brother has been identified as Jaques de Boys. Rosalind, who is sometimes called Rosaline in the folio, is consistently Rosalind here. Those few substantive changes that are listed below generally follow generations of editorial practice. The adopted reading in italics is followed by the folio reading in roman.

I.1 41 *Ay* I (thus throughout)   104 *she* hee   152 *OLIVER* (not in F)

I.2 3 *I* (not in F)   51 *and* (not in F)   79 *CELIA* Ros[alind]   87 *Le Beau* the Beu

I.3 55 *likelihood* likelihoods   76 *her* per   94 *lacks then* lacks thou then   135 *we in* in we

II.1 49 *much* must   59 *of the country* of Countrie

II.3 10 *some* seeme   16 *ORLANDO* (not in F)   29 *ORLANDO* Ad[am]   58 *meed* (some copies of F read "neede")   71 *seventeen* seauentie

II.4 s.d. *dressed as* for   35 *Wearying* Wearing   41 *thy wound* they would   67 *you* your

II.5 1 *AMIENS* (not in F)   39–40 *Here . . . weather* (F reads "Heere shall he see, &c.")   44 *JACQUES* Amy[ens]

II.7 55 *Not to* (not in F)   64 *sin . . . sin* fin . . . fin   87 *comes* come   173 *AMIENS* (not in F)   181 *Then* The   197 *master* masters

III.2 11 *Master* Mr   83 *Master* Mr   114 *graft* graffe   122 *a* (not in F)   142 *her* his   155 *How now? Back, friends.* How now backe friends: 232 *such* (not in F)   239 *thy* the   241 *heart* Hart   252 *b' wi'* buy   351 *deifying* defying   359 *are* art

III.3 19 *it* (not in F)   68 *Master* Mr   88 *TOUCHSTONE* Ol.   89 *Master* Mr

III.4 28 *a* (not in F)   40 *puny* puisny

III.5 128 *I* (not in F)

IV.1 1 *be* (not in F)   17 *which* in which   27 *travel* travaile   29 *b' wi* buy   45 *heart-whole* heart hole   145 *hyena* Hyen   197 *in, it* in, in

IV.2 2 *[FIRST] LORD* Lord   7 *[SECOND] LORD* Lord

IV.3 5 s.d. *Enter Silvius* (follows l.3 in F)   141 *In* I   154 *his* this

V.1 22 *Wast* Was't   36 *sir* sit   54–55 *policy* police

V.2 7 *her* (not in F)   30–31 *overcame* overcome   60 *heart* hart

V.3 14 s.d. *Both Pages sing* Song.   18 *In* In the; *ringtime* rang time   29–32 *And . . . springtime, etc.* (follows l.20 in F)   39 *b' wi'* buy

V.4 34 s.d. *Enter . . . Audrey* (follows l.33 in F)   80 *to the* ro   130 *heart . . . heart* hart . . . hart   138 s.d. *All sing* Song.   148 s.d., 149 *JAQUES DE BOYS* Second Brother   162 *them* him   169 *were* vvete   181 *JAQUES DE BOYS* 2. Brother

As You Like It

[NAMES OF THE ACTORS

DUKE SENIOR, *in banishment*
DUKE FREDERICK, *his brother and usurper*
AMIENS ⎫
JAQUES ⎭ *lords attending on Duke Senior*
OLIVER, *eldest son of Sir Rowland de Boys*
JAQUES ⎫
ORLANDO ⎭ *younger sons of Sir Rowland de Boys*
LE BEAU, *a courtier attending on Duke Frederick*
CHARLES, *a wrestler at the court*
ADAM, *an old servant to Sir Rowland de Boys*
DENNIS, *a servant to Oliver*
TOUCHSTONE, *a clown*
SIR OLIVER MARTEXT, *a country curate*
CORIN ⎫
SILVIUS ⎭ *shepherds*
WILLIAM, *a country fellow*
HYMEN, *god of marriage*
ROSALIND, *daughter of Duke Senior*
CELIA, *daughter of Duke Frederick*
PHEBE, *a shepherdess*
AUDREY, *a country wench*
LORDS, PAGES, AND ATTENDANTS

SCENE: *Oliver's orchard; Duke Frederick's court;*
the Forest of Arden]
*

As You Like It

ᴈ I.1 *Enter Orlando and Adam.*

ORLANDO As I remember, Adam, it was upon this fashion bequeathed me by will but poor a thousand   2
crowns, and, as thou sayest, charged my brother on his
blessing to breed me well: and there begins my sadness.
My brother Jaques he keeps at school, and report   5
speaks goldenly of his profit. For my part, he keeps me   6
rustically at home or, to speak more properly, stays me   7
here at home unkept: for call you that keeping for a
gentleman of my birth that differs not from the stalling
of an ox? His horses are bred better, for, besides that   10
they are fair with their feeding, they are taught their   11
manage, and to that end riders dearly hired; but I, his   12
brother, gain nothing under him but growth, for the
which his animals on his dunghills are as much bound
to him as I. Besides this nothing that he so plentifully
gives me, the something that nature gave me his coun-   16
tenance seems to take from me: he lets me feed with his
hinds, bars me the place of a brother, and, as much as   18
in him lies, mines my gentility with my education. This   19

I.1 The garden of Oliver's manor house 2 *but poor* merely 5 *Jaques* (this
name is pronounced "jakes," calling to mind a common word for a privy, or,
when the meter requires it to be pronounced as two syllables, "jaykus" or
"jaykwis") 6 *profit* progress; *keeps* maintains 7 *stays* detains 11 *fair with
their feeding* beautiful because so well fed 12 *manage* actions and paces;
dearly at great expense 16–17 *countenance* attitude 18 *hinds* farmhands;
bars me shuts me out of 19 *mines* undermines

20   is it, Adam, that grieves me; and the spirit of my father,
     which I think is within me, begins to mutiny against
     this servitude. I will no longer endure it, though yet I
     know no wise remedy how to avoid it.
        Enter Oliver.
     ADAM   Yonder comes my master, your brother.
     ORLANDO   Go apart, Adam, and thou shalt hear how he
26   will shake me up.
27   OLIVER   Now, sir, what make you here?
     ORLANDO   Nothing. I am not taught to make anything.
     OLIVER   What mar you then, sir?
30   ORLANDO   Marry, sir, I am helping you to mar that
     which God made, a poor unworthy brother of yours,
     with idleness.
33   OLIVER   Marry, sir, be better employed, and be naught
     awhile.
35   ORLANDO   Shall I keep your hogs and eat husks with
     them? What prodigal portion have I spent that I should
     come to such penury?
     OLIVER   Know you where you are, sir?
39   ORLANDO   O, sir, very well: here in your orchard.
40   OLIVER   Know you before whom, sir?
     ORLANDO   Ay, better than him I am before knows me. I
42   know you are my eldest brother, and in the gentle con-
43   dition of blood you should so know me. The courtesy
     of nations allows you my better in that you are the first
     born, but the same tradition takes not away my blood
     were there twenty brothers betwixt us. I have as much

---

26 *shake me up* harass me   27 *make* do (but Orlando also takes it in the
sense of "create")   30 *Marry* why, indeed (originally an oath on the name of
the Virgin Mary)   33 *be naught* shut up, get lost   35–36 *eat . . . portion* (alluding to the Prodigal Son, who wasted his inheritance and then had to eat
with the pigs; see Luke 15:11–32)   39 *orchard* garden   42–43 *gentle . . .
blood* bond of family loyalty   43-44 *courtesy of nations* recognized custom
(of primogeniture, by which the first son inherited control of the estate, and
the title, if there was one)

of my father in me as you, albeit I confess your coming   47
before me is nearer to his reverence.   48

OLIVER What, boy!
    [Strikes him.]

ORLANDO Come, come, elder brother, you are too   50
young in this.
    [Seizes him.]

OLIVER Wilt thou lay hands on me, villain?   52

ORLANDO I am no villain. I am the youngest son of Sir
Rowland de Boys; he was my father, and he is thrice a
villain that says such a father begot villains. Wert thou
not my brother, I would not take this hand from thy
throat till this other had pulled out thy tongue for saying so. Thou hast railed on thyself.   58

ADAM Sweet masters, be patient: for your father's re-
membrance, be at accord.   60

OLIVER Let me go, I say.

ORLANDO I will not till I please. You shall hear me. My
father charged you in his will to give me good education: you have trained me like a peasant, obscuring and
hiding from me all gentlemanlike qualities. The spirit   65
of my father grows strong in me, and I will no longer
endure it: therefore allow me such exercises as may be-   67
come a gentleman, or give me the poor allottery my fa-   68
ther left me by testament; with that I will go buy my   69
fortunes.   70
    [Releases him.]

OLIVER And what wilt thou do? beg when that is spent?
Well, sir, get you in. I will not long be troubled with

---

47 *coming* being born 48 *nearer . . . reverence* brings you closer to his social
position 52 *villain* (1) peasant or someone of low birth, (2) scoundrel (in
the following lines, Orlando plays on the two meanings) 58 *railed on* ver-
bally abused 65 *qualities* accomplishments 67 *exercises* activities (such as
sports and education) 68 *allottery* allotment or inheritance 69 *testament*
(their father's will)

you. You shall have some part of your will. I pray you leave me.

ORLANDO   I will no further offend you than becomes me for my good.

OLIVER   Get you with him, you old dog.

ADAM   Is "old dog" my reward? Most true, I have lost my teeth in your service. God be with my old master; he
80   would not have spoke such a word.

                                        Exeunt Orlando, Adam.

81   OLIVER   Is it even so? Begin you to grow upon me? I will
82   physic your rankness and yet give no thousand crowns neither. Holla, Dennis!

        Enter Dennis.

DENNIS   Calls your worship?

OLIVER   Was not Charles the duke's wrestler here to speak with me?

87   DENNIS   So please you, he is here at the door and impor- tunes access to you.

OLIVER   Call him in. *[Exit Dennis.]* 'Twill be a good way;
90   and tomorrow the wrestling is.

        Enter Charles.

CHARLES   Good morrow to your worship.

OLIVER   Good Monsieur Charles, what's the new news at the new court?

CHARLES   There's no news at the court, sir, but the old news: that is, the old duke is banished by his younger brother the new duke, and three or four loving lords have put themselves into voluntary exile with him, whose lands and revenues enrich the new duke; there- fore he gives them good leave to wander.

100   OLIVER   Can you tell if Rosalind, the duke's daughter, be banished with her father?

CHARLES   O, no; for the duke's daughter her cousin so loves her, being ever from their cradles bred together,

---

81 *grow upon me* i.e., encroach on my place   82 *physic* cure; *rankness* exuber- ant growth (cf. l. 81)   87–88 *importunes* pleads for

that she would have followed her exile, or have died to
stay behind her. She is at the court, and no less beloved
of her uncle than his own daughter, and never two
ladies loved as they do.

OLIVER Where will the old duke live?

CHARLES They say he is already in the Forest of Arden,
and a many merry men with him; and there they live   110
like the old Robin Hood of England. They say many   111
young gentlemen flock to him every day, and fleet the   112
time carelessly as they did in the golden world.   113

OLIVER What, you wrestle tomorrow before the new
duke?

CHARLES Marry do I, sir; and I came to acquaint you
with a matter. I am given, sir, secretly to understand
that your younger brother, Orlando, hath a disposition
to come in disguised against me to try a fall. Tomorrow,   119
sir, I wrestle for my credit, and he that escapes me with-   120
out some broken limb shall acquit him well. Your
brother is but young and tender, and for your love I
would be loath to foil him, as I must for my own honor   123
if he come in: therefore, out of my love to you, I came
hither to acquaint you withal, that either you might   125
stay him from his intendment, or brook such disgrace   126
well as he shall run into, in that it is a thing of his own
search and altogether against my will.   128

OLIVER Charles, I thank thee for thy love to me, which
thou shalt find I will most kindly requite. I had myself   130
notice of my brother's purpose herein and have by un-   131
derhand means labored to dissuade him from it; but he

---

111 *Robin Hood* a legendary figure who was said to haunt Sherwood Forest
with his band of "merry men," robbing from the rich to give to the poor
112 *fleet* pass 113 *golden world* the "once upon a time" of classical mythology, when humankind ate abundantly without struggle, and enjoyed peace,
prosperity, innocence, and eternal spring (see Ovid, *Metamorphoses,* Book I)
119 *fall* bout 120 *credit* reputation 123 *foil* throw 125 *withal* with this
126 *stay* prevent; *intendment* intention; *brook* accept 128 *search* seeking
131–32 *underhand* indirect

133 is resolute. I'll tell thee, Charles, it is the stubbornest young fellow of France; full of ambition, an envious emulator of every man's good parts, a secret and villainous contriver against me his natural brother: therefore use thy discretion. I had as lief thou didst break his neck as his finger. And thou wert best look to't; for if thou dost him any slight disgrace, or if he do not

140 mightily grace himself on thee, he will practice against thee by poison, entrap thee by some treacherous device, and never leave thee till he hath ta'en thy life by some indirect means or other; for I assure thee, and almost with tears I speak it, there is not one so young and so villainous this day living. I speak but brotherly of him,

146 but should I anatomize him to thee as he is, I must blush and weep, and thou must look pale and wonder.

CHARLES I am heartily glad I came hither to you. If he

149 come tomorrow, I'll give him his payment. If ever he go

150 alone again, I'll never wrestle for prize more. And so God keep your worship.

OLIVER Farewell, good Charles. *Exit [Charles]*. Now will

153 I stir this gamester. I hope I shall see an end of him; for my soul, yet I know not why, hates nothing more than

155 he. Yet he's gentle, never schooled and yet learned, full

156 of noble device, of all sorts enchantingly beloved; and indeed so much in the heart of the world, and especially of my own people, who best know him, that I am

159 altogether misprised. But it shall not be so long: this

160 wrestler shall clear all. Nothing remains but that I kindle the boy thither, which now I'll go about. *Exit.*

*

---

133 *it* he   140 *grace himself on thee* gain credit at your expense; *practice* plot
146 *anatomize* dissect, describe   149–50 *go alone* walk without help   153
gamester player, athlete, joker (of Orlando)   155 *gentle* having the qualities
of a gentleman   156 *device* designs; *sorts* social classes; *enchantingly* as if they
had been bewitched by him   159 *misprised* unappreciated

❧ **I.2** *Enter Rosalind and Celia.*

CELIA I pray thee, Rosalind, sweet my coz, be merry.   1

ROSALIND Dear Celia, I show more mirth than I am
mistress of, and would you yet I were merrier? Unless
you could teach me to forget a banished father, you
must not learn me how to remember any extraordinary   5
pleasure.

CELIA Herein I see thou lovest me not with the full
weight that I love thee. If my uncle, thy banished father, had banished thy uncle, the duke my father, so
thou hadst been still with me, I could have taught my   10
love to take thy father for mine. So wouldst thou, if the
truth of thy love to me were so righteously tempered as   12
mine is to thee.

ROSALIND Well, I will forget the condition of my estate 14
to rejoice in yours.

CELIA You know my father hath no child but I, nor
none is like to have; and truly, when he dies, thou shalt
be his heir; for what he hath taken away from thy father
perforce, I will render thee again in affection. By mine   19
honor, I will, and when I break that oath, let me turn   20
monster. Therefore, my sweet Rose, my dear Rose, be
merry.

ROSALIND From henceforth I will, coz, and devise
sports. Let me see, what think you of falling in love?   24

CELIA Marry, I prithee do, to make sport withal; but   25
love no man in good earnest, nor no further in sport
neither than with safety of a pure blush thou mayst in   27
honor come off again.   28

I.2 The grounds of Duke Frederick's palace **1** *coz* cousin (or, more generally, kinswoman) **5** *learn* teach **12** *righteously tempered* perfectly balanced
14 *condition . . . estate* my situation **19** *perforce* forcibly **24** *sports* diver-
sions **25** *withal* with **27** *pure* innocent **28** *come off* get away

ROSALIND What shall be our sport then?

30 CELIA Let us sit and mock the good housewife Fortune
from her wheel, that her gifts may henceforth be be-
stowed equally.

ROSALIND I would we could do so, for her benefits are
mightily misplaced, and the bountiful blind woman
doth most mistake in her gifts to women.

CELIA 'Tis true, for those that she makes fair she scarce
37 makes honest, and those that she makes honest she
38 makes very ill-favoredly.

39 ROSALIND Nay, now thou goest from Fortune's office to
40 Nature's. Fortune reigns in gifts of the world, not in the
41 lineaments of Nature.
        Enter [Touchstone the] Clown.

CELIA No; when Nature hath made a fair creature, may
she not by Fortune fall into the fire? Though Nature
hath given us wit to flout at Fortune, hath not Fortune
sent in this fool to cut off the argument?

ROSALIND Indeed, there is Fortune too hard for Nature
47 when Fortune makes Nature's natural the cutter-off of
Nature's wit.

CELIA Peradventure this is not Fortune's work neither,
50 but Nature's, who perceiveth our natural wits too dull
to reason of such goddesses and hath sent this natural
52 for our whetstone, for always the dullness of the fool is
53 the whetstone of the wits. How now, wit; whither wander you?

30–31 *good . . . wheel* (Celia compares the blind goddess Fortune, who spins
a "wheel of fortune" by which some rise as others fall, to a housewife at her
spinning wheel) **37** *honest* chaste **38** *ill-favoredly* ugly **39** *office* job, turf
39–41 *Nay . . . Nature* (Fortune controls whether we are rich, powerful, or
beloved, while Nature controls physical appearance) **40** *reigns in* presides
over **41** *lineaments* features **41 s.d.** *Touchstone* (his name means a kind of
flint used to test the purity of gold and silver) **47** *natural* born fool **52**
whetstone stone for sharpening tools – i.e., a sharpener **53–54** *wit . . . wan-*
der (proverbial expression usually used in reference to a person who had wan-
dered off the subject)

TOUCHSTONE   Mistress, you must come away to your father.

CELIA   Were you made the messenger?

TOUCHSTONE   No, by mine honor, but I was bid to come
for you.

ROSALIND   Where learned you that oath, fool?   60

TOUCHSTONE   Of a certain knight that swore by his honor
they were good pancakes, and swore by his honor the
mustard was naught. Now I'll stand to it, the pancakes   63
were naught, and the mustard was good, and yet was not   64
the knight forsworn.   65

CELIA   How prove you that in the great heap of your
knowledge?

ROSALIND   Ay, marry, now unmuzzle your wisdom.

TOUCHSTONE   Stand you both forth now. Stroke your
chins, and swear by your beards that I am a knave.   70

CELIA   By our beards, if we had them, thou art.

TOUCHSTONE   By my knavery, if I had it, then I were;
but if you swear by that that is not, you are not for-   73
sworn; no more was this knight, swearing by his honor,
for he never had any; or if he had, he had sworn it away
before ever he saw those pancakes or that mustard.

CELIA   Prithee, who is't that thou meanest?

TOUCHSTONE   One that old Frederick, your father, loves.

CELIA   My father's love is enough to honor him enough:
speak no more of him; you'll be whipped for taxation   80
one of these days.

TOUCHSTONE   The more pity that fools may not speak
wisely what wise men do foolishly.

CELIA   By my troth, thou sayest true, for since the little
wit that fools have was silenced, the little foolery that
wise men have makes a great show. Here comes Monsieur Le Beau.

63, 64 *naught* bad (with a pun on "nought," worthless) 65 *forsworn* falsely
sworn   70 *knave* (1) servant, (2) dishonest or troublesome person (Touchstone is certainly the former, and arguably the latter) 73 *that ... not* i.e.,
their beards   80 *taxation* slander

Enter Le Beau.

ROSALIND   With his mouth full of news.

89 CELIA   Which he will put on us as pigeons feed their
90   young.

ROSALIND   Then shall we be news-crammed.

92 CELIA   All the better; we shall be the more marketable.

93   *Bonjour*, Monsieur Le Beau, what's the news?

LE BEAU   Fair princess, you have lost much good sport.

95 CELIA   Sport; of what color?

LE BEAU   What color, madam? How shall I answer you?

97 ROSALIND   As wit and fortune will.

98 TOUCHSTONE   Or as the destinies decree.

99 CELIA   Well said; that was laid on with a trowel.

100 TOUCHSTONE   Nay, if I keep not my rank –

ROSALIND   Thou losest thy old smell.

102 LE BEAU   You amaze me, ladies. I would have told you of
good wrestling, which you have lost the sight of.

ROSALIND   Yet tell us the manner of the wrestling.

LE BEAU   I will tell you the beginning; and if it please
your ladyships, you may see the end, for the best is yet
to do, and here, where you are, they are coming to perform it.

CELIA   Well, the beginning that is dead and buried.

110 LE BEAU   There comes an old man and his three sons.

CELIA   I could match this beginning with an old tale.

112 LE BEAU   Three proper young men, of excellent growth
and presence.

114 ROSALIND   With bills on their necks, "Be it known unto
115   all men by these presents."

LE BEAU   The eldest of the three wrestled with Charles,
the duke's wrestler; which Charles in a moment threw

---

89 *put on* force upon   92 *marketable* i.e., because plumper   93 *Bonjour*
good day (French)   95 *color* sort   97 *will* determine   98 *destinies* in Greek
mythology, the three goddesses, or Fates, who spin out the texture and
length of each human life   99 *with a trowel* i.e., slapped on thickly   100
rank (1) reputation as a witty person, (2) stink   102 *amaze* confuse   112
proper handsome   114 *bills* notices   115 *presents* legal documents

him and broke three of his ribs, that there is little hope   118
of life in him. So he served the second, and so the third.
Yonder they lie, the poor old man, their father, making   120
such pitiful dole over them that all the beholders take   121
his part with weeping.

ROSALIND Alas!

TOUCHSTONE But what is the sport, monsieur, that the
ladies have lost?

LE BEAU Why, this that I speak of.

TOUCHSTONE Thus men may grow wiser every day. It is
the first time that ever I heard breaking of ribs was
sport for ladies.

CELIA Or I, I promise thee.   130

ROSALIND But is there any else longs to see this broken   131
music in his sides? Is there yet another dotes upon rib-
breaking? Shall we see this wrestling, cousin?

LE BEAU You must, if you stay here, for here is the place
appointed for the wrestling, and they are ready to perform it.

CELIA Yonder sure they are coming. Let us now stay and
see it.   138

    Flourish. Enter Duke [Frederick], Lords, Orlando,
    Charles, and Attendants.

DUKE FREDERICK Come on. Since the youth will not be   139
entreated, his own peril on his forwardness.   140

ROSALIND Is yonder the man?

LE BEAU Even he, madam.

CELIA Alas, he is too young; yet he looks successfully.   143

DUKE FREDERICK How now, daughter and cousin; are   144
you crept hither to see the wrestling?

ROSALIND Ay, my liege, so please you give us leave.

---

118 *that* so that 121 *dole* lament 131–32 *broken music* the wheezing
caused by broken ribs (literally, music written in parts for different instru-
ments) 138 s.d. *Flourish* trumpet fanfare (to announce the duke's entrance)
139–40 *Since . . . forwardness* since Orlando cannot be talked out of
wrestling, he will have to take his lumps 140 *entreated* dissuaded; *forward-*
ness rashness 143 *successfully* likely to succeed 144 *cousin* kinswoman

DUKE FREDERICK   You will take little delight in it, I can
148   tell you, there is such odds in the man. In pity of the
149   challenger's youth I would fain dissuade him, but he
150   will not be entreated. Speak to him, ladies; see if you
can move him.
CELIA   Call him hither, good Monsieur Le Beau.
DUKE FREDERICK   Do so. I'll not be by.
   [Steps aside.]
LE BEAU   Monsieur the challenger, the princess calls for
you.
ORLANDO   I attend them with all respect and duty.
ROSALIND   Young man, have you challenged Charles the
wrestler?
ORLANDO   No, fair princess. He is the general chal-
160   lenger; I come but in as others do, to try with him the
strength of my youth.
CELIA   Young gentleman, your spirits are too bold for
your years. You have seen cruel proof of this man's
164   strength; if you saw yourself with your eyes or knew
yourself with your judgment, the fear of your adven-
166   ture would counsel you to a more equal enterprise. We
pray you for your own sake to embrace your own safety
and give over this attempt.
ROSALIND   Do, young sir. Your reputation shall not
170   therefore be misprised; we will make it our suit to the
duke that the wrestling might not go forward.
ORLANDO   I beseech you, punish me not with your hard
thoughts, wherein I confess me much guilty to deny so
fair and excellent ladies anything. But let your fair eyes
and gentle wishes go with me to my trial; wherein if I
176   be foiled, there is but one shamed that was never gra-
cious; if killed, but one dead that is willing to be so. I

---

148 *odds* superiority   149 *fain* gladly   164–65 *if . . . judgment* if you could
see how you look, or accurately assess your chances   166 *equal enterprise*
even match   170 *misprised* undervalued   176 *foiled* defeated   176–77 *gra-
cious* blessed, fortunate

shall do my friends no wrong, for I have none to
lament me; the world no injury, for in it I have nothing. Only in the world I fill up a place, which may be   *180*
better supplied when I have made it empty.

ROSALIND   The little strength that I have, I would it were
with you.

CELIA   And mine to eke out hers.   184

ROSALIND   Fare you well. Pray heaven I be deceived in   185
you!

CELIA   Your heart's desires be with you!

CHARLES   Come, where is this young gallant that is so
desirous to lie with his mother earth?   189

ORLANDO   Ready, sir; but his will hath in it a more mod- 190
est working.   191

DUKE FREDERICK   You shall try but one fall.

CHARLES   No, I warrant your grace you shall not entreat
him to a second that have so mightily persuaded him
from a first.

ORLANDO   You mean to mock me after. You should not
have mocked me before. But come your ways.   197

ROSALIND   Now Hercules be thy speed, young man!   198

CELIA   I would I were invisible, to catch the strong fellow
by the leg.   *200*

   Wrestle.

ROSALIND   O excellent young man!

CELIA   If I had a thunderbolt in mine eye, I can tell who   202
should down.

   [Charles is thrown.] Shout.

DUKE FREDERICK   No more, no more.

---

184 *eke out* add to   185–86 *deceived in you* mistaken in my view of your
abilities   189 *lie . . . earth* take a fall (with the connotations both of being
buried in and having sex with the earth)   190 *will* desire   191 *working* un-
dertaking   197 *come your ways* come on   198 *Hercules* in Greek mythology,
a hero of great strength, who included among his feats a successful wrestling
match against the giant Antaeus; *be thy speed* favor you   202 *If . . . eye* if I
could cast a thunderbolt with my eyes

205 ORLANDO   Yes, I beseech your grace; I am not yet well
breathed.

DUKE FREDERICK
How dost thou, Charles?

LE BEAU   He cannot speak, my lord.

DUKE FREDERICK
Bear him away.
     [Charles is borne out.]
               What is thy name, young man?

   ORLANDO   Orlando, my liege, the youngest son of Sir
210 Rowland de Boys.

DUKE FREDERICK
I would thou hadst been son to some man else.
The world esteemed thy father honorable,
213 But I did find him still mine enemy.
Thou shouldst have better pleased me with this deed
215 Hadst thou descended from another house.
But fare thee well; thou art a gallant youth;
I would thou hadst told me of another father.
               Exit Duke [, with train].

CELIA
Were I my father, coz, would I do this?

ORLANDO
I am more proud to be Sir Rowland's son,
220 His youngest son, and would not change that calling
To be adopted heir to Frederick.

ROSALIND
My father loved Sir Rowland as his soul,
And all the world was of my father's mind.
Had I before known this young man his son,
225 I should have given him tears unto entreaties
Ere he should thus have ventured.

CELIA   Gentle cousin,
Let us go thank him and encourage him.

205–6 *well breathed* warmed up   213 *still* constantly   215 *house* family
220 *calling* social position   225 *unto* on top of

My father's rough and envious disposition
Sticks me at heart. Sir, you have well deserved;
If you do keep your promises in love   230
But justly as you have exceeded all promise,   231
Your mistress shall be happy.
ROSALIND   Gentleman,
    [Gives chain.]
Wear this for me, one out of suits with fortune,   233
That could give more but that her hand lacks means.   234
Shall we go, coz?
CELIA   Ay. Fare you well, fair gentleman.
ORLANDO
Can I not say "I thank you"? My better parts   236
Are all thrown down, and that which here stands up
Is but a quintain, a mere lifeless block.   238
ROSALIND
He calls us back. My pride fell with my fortunes;
I'll ask him what he would. Did you call, sir?   240
Sir, you have wrestled well, and overthrown
More than your enemies.
CELIA   Will you go, coz?
ROSALIND
Have with you. Fare you well.   *Exit [with Celia].*   243
ORLANDO
What passion hangs these weights upon my tongue?
I cannot speak to her, yet she urged conference.   245
    Enter Le Beau.
O poor Orlando, thou art overthrown!
Or Charles or something weaker masters thee.   247
LE BEAU
Good sir, I do in friendship counsel you
To leave this place. Albeit you have deserved

---

231 *But justly* exactly   233 *suits* favor   234 *could* would   236 *parts* attributes   238 *quintain* wooden post used in practicing tilting and jousting, de-
cidedly elite sports (Orlando emphasizes that he stands as speechless as a
post; he may also refer to having an erection)   243 *Have with you* come on
245 *urged conference* invited conversation   247 *Or . . . or* either . . . or

250 High commendation, true applause, and love,
251 Yet such is now the duke's condition
252 That he misconsters all that you have done.
253 The duke is humorous. What he is, indeed,
254 More suits you to conceive than I to speak of.

ORLANDO
I thank you, sir; and pray you tell me this:
Which of the two was daughter of the duke,
That here was at the wrestling?

LE BEAU
Neither his daughter, if we judge by manners,
259 But yet indeed the taller is his daughter,
260 The other is daughter to the banished duke,
And here detained by her usurping uncle
262 To keep his daughter company, whose loves
Are dearer than the natural bond of sisters.
But I can tell you that of late this duke
Hath ta'en displeasure 'gainst his gentle niece,
266 Grounded upon no other argument
But that the people praise her for her virtues
And pity her for her good father's sake;
And, on my life, his malice 'gainst the lady
270 Will suddenly break forth. Sir, fare you well.
271 Hereafter, in a better world than this,
I shall desire more love and knowledge of you.

ORLANDO
I rest much bounden to you. Fare you well.
[Exit Le Beau.]
274 Thus must I from the smoke into the smother,

---

251 *condition* disposition 252 *misconsters* misconstrues 253 *humorous* moody (as a result of an imbalance of the "humors," or fluids, of which the body was thought to be composed) 254 *conceive* imagine 259 *taller* (either Le Beau or Shakespeare is confused here; Rosalind later claims to be the taller [I.3.113]) 262 *loves* i.e., for each other 266 *argument* reason 271 *world* state of affairs 274 *must I* must I go; *smother* heavy smoke (as in the proverbial expression "out of the frying pan, into the fire")

From tyrant duke unto a tyrant brother.
But heavenly Rosalind!   *Exit.*

                              *

🙌 **I.3** *Enter Celia and Rosalind.*

CELIA   Why, cousin, why, Rosalind! Cupid have mercy,
not a word?

ROSALIND   Not one to throw at a dog.

CELIA   No, thy words are too precious to be cast away
upon curs; throw some of them at me; come, lame me   5
with reasons.

ROSALIND   Then there were two cousins laid up, when
the one should be lamed with reasons and the other
mad without any.

CELIA   But is all this for your father?   10

ROSALIND   No, some of it is for my child's father. O, how
full of briers is this working-day world!

CELIA   They are but burrs, cousin, thrown upon thee in
holiday foolery; if we walk not in the trodden paths,
our very petticoats will catch them.

ROSALIND   I could shake them off my coat; these burrs
are in my heart.

CELIA   Hem them away.   18

ROSALIND   I would try, if I could cry "hem," and have   19
him.   20

CELIA   Come, come, wrestle with thy affections.

ROSALIND   O, they take the part of a better wrestler than
myself!

CELIA   O, a good wish upon you! You will try in time, in   24
despite of a fall. But turning these jests out of service,   25
let us talk in good earnest. Is it possible on such a sud-

I.3 Duke Frederick's palace   **5–6** *lame me with reasons* pelt me with words
18 *Hem* (1) clear the throat of phlegm or a "frog," (2) mend   **19** *cry "hem"*
clear the throat (as in saying "ahem")   **24** *try* test your love   **25** *despite . . .
fall* even if it requires a wrestling match or sexual intercourse; *turning . . . service* putting these jokes aside

den you should fall into so strong a liking with old Sir
Rowland's youngest son?

ROSALIND   The duke my father loved his father dearly.

30 CELIA   Doth it therefore ensue that you should love his
31 son dearly? By this kind of chase, I should hate him, for
my father hated his father dearly; yet I hate not Orlando.

ROSALIND   No, faith, hate him not, for my sake.

35 CELIA   Why should I not? Doth he not deserve well?

Enter Duke [Frederick], with Lords.

ROSALIND   Let me love him for that, and do you love
him because I do. Look, here comes the duke.

CELIA   With his eyes full of anger.

DUKE FREDERICK

39 Mistress, dispatch you with your safest haste
40 And get you from our court.

ROSALIND   Me, uncle?

DUKE FREDERICK   You, cousin.
Within these ten days if that thou beest found
So near our public court as twenty miles,
Thou diest for it.

ROSALIND   I do beseech your grace
Let me the knowledge of my fault bear with me.

45 If with myself I hold intelligence
Or have acquaintance with mine own desires,

47 If that I do not dream or be not frantic,
As I do trust I am not; then, dear uncle,
Never so much as in a thought unborn

50 Did I offend your highness.

DUKE FREDERICK   Thus do all traitors.

51 If their purgation did consist in words,

---

31 *chase* logic   35 *deserve well* i.e., to be hated (but Rosalind ignores the im-
plied conclusion)   39 *safest haste* i.e., the hastier the safer   45 *hold intelligence* am in communication   47 *frantic* insane   51 *purgation* exoneration

They are as innocent as grace itself.   52
Let it suffice thee that I trust thee not.

ROSALIND
Yet your mistrust cannot make me a traitor.
Tell me whereon the likelihood depends.   55

DUKE FREDERICK
Thou art thy father's daughter, there's enough.

ROSALIND
So was I when your highness took his dukedom;
So was I when your highness banished him.
Treason is not inherited, my lord,
Or if we did derive it from our friends,   60
What's that to me? My father was no traitor.
Then, good my liege, mistake me not so much   62
To think my poverty is treacherous.

CELIA
Dear sovereign, hear me speak.

DUKE FREDERICK
Ay, Celia. We stayed her for your sake,   65
Else had she with her father ranged along.   66

CELIA
I did not then entreat to have her stay;
It was your pleasure and your own remorse.   68
I was too young that time to value her,   69
But now I know her. If she be a traitor,   70
Why, so am I. We still have slept together,   71
Rose at an instant, learned, played, eat together;
And wheresoe'er we went, like Juno's swans,   73
Still we went coupled and inseparable.

---

52 *grace* divine benevolence   55 *whereon . . . depends* the grounds of your
suspicion   60 *friends* relations   62 *mistake . . . much* do not so misunder-
stand   65 *stayed* kept at court   66 *ranged along* been banished   68 *remorse*
pity, compassion   69 *that time* then   71 *still* always   73 *Juno's swans* two
swans who pulled Juno's chariot (according to Ovid, it was Venus who was
drawn through the air by a pair of swans)

DUKE FREDERICK
75   She is too subtle for thee; and her smoothness,
        Her very silence and her patience,
        Speak to the people, and they pity her.
        Thou art a fool. She robs thee of thy name,
79   And thou wilt show more bright and seem more vir-
            tuous
80   When she is gone. Then open not thy lips.
81   Firm and irrevocable is my doom
        Which I have passed upon her; she is banished.

CELIA
        Pronounce that sentence then on me, my liege;
        I cannot live out of her company.

DUKE FREDERICK
        You are a fool. You, niece, provide yourself;
86   If you outstay the time, upon mine honor,
87   And in the greatness of my word, you die.
                            Exit Duke [Frederick, with Lords].

CELIA
        O my poor Rosalind, whither wilt thou go?
        Wilt thou change fathers? I will give thee mine.
90   I charge thee be not thou more grieved than I am.

ROSALIND
        I have more cause.

CELIA   Thou hast not, cousin.
        Prithee be cheerful. Know'st thou not the duke
        Hath banished me, his daughter?

ROSALIND   That he hath not.

CELIA
        No? hath not? Rosalind lacks then the love
        Which teacheth thee that thou and I am one.
        Shall we be sundered, shall we part, sweet girl?
        No, let my father seek another heir.

---

75 *subtle* crafty   79 *virtuous* admirable   81 *doom* judgment   86 *time* i.e.,
the ten-day limit he has imposed   87 *greatness* authority

Therefore devise with me how we may fly,   98
Whither to go, and what to bear with us;
And do not seek to take your change upon you,   100
To bear your griefs yourself and leave me out;
For, by this heaven, now at our sorrows pale,   102
Say what thou canst, I'll go along with thee.

ROSALIND
Why, whither shall we go?

CELIA
To seek my uncle in the Forest of Arden.

ROSALIND
Alas, what danger will it be to us,
Maids as we are, to travel forth so far!
Beauty provoketh thieves sooner than gold.

CELIA
I'll put myself in poor and mean attire   109
And with a kind of umber smirch my face;   110
The like do you; so shall we pass along
And never stir assailants.   112

ROSALIND   Were it not better,
Because that I am more than common tall,
That I did suit me all points like a man?   114
A gallant curtal ax upon my thigh,   115
A boarspear in my hand; and, in my heart
Lie there what hidden woman's fear there will,
We'll have a swashing and a martial outside,   118
As many other mannish cowards have   119
That do outface it with their semblances.   120

CELIA
What shall I call thee when thou art a man?

---

98 *devise* plan   100 *change* i.e., of fortunes   102 *at . . . pale* turned pale by
our sorrows   109 *mean* humble, shabby   110 *umber* brown dirt   112 *stir*
provoke   114 *suit me all points* dress completely   115 *curtal ax* cutlass – a
short, curving sword   118 *swashing* blustering   119 *mannish* i.e., pretending manliness   120 *outface it* bluff it out; *semblances* false fronts

ROSALIND
    I'll have no worse a name than Jove's own page,
123   And therefore look you call me Ganymede.
    But what will you be called?

CELIA
    Something that hath a reference to my state:
126   No longer Celia, but Aliena.

ROSALIND
127   But, cousin, what if we assayed to steal
    The clownish fool out of your father's court;
    Would he not be a comfort to our travel?

CELIA
130   He'll go along o'er the wide world with me;
131   Leave me alone to woo him. Let's away
    And get our jewels and our wealth together,
    Devise the fittest time and safest way
    To hide us from pursuit that will be made
    After my flight. Now go we in content
    To liberty, and not to banishment.   *Exeunt.*

*

❧ **II.1** *Enter Duke Senior, Amiens, and two or three*
     Lords, [dressed as] Foresters.

DUKE SENIOR
    Now, my co-mates and brothers in exile,
    Hath not old custom made this life more sweet
3   Than that of painted pomp? Are not these woods
    More free from peril than the envious court?

---

123 *look you* be sure to; *Ganymede* in classical mythology, a beautiful young
man whom Jove, the king of the gods, made his cupbearer (the name was
often used more generally, to refer to a young man who served an older man
sexually) **126** *Aliena* i.e., strange or estranged **127** *assayed* undertook
131 *woo* coax
    II.1 The Forest of Arden **s.d.** *Foresters* those who dwell in the forest
(rather than the court) **3** *painted pomp* false splendor (of the court)

Here feel we not the penalty of Adam;   5
The seasons' difference, as the icy fang   6
And churlish chiding of the winter's wind,   7
Which, when it bites and blows upon my body
Even till I shrink with cold, I smile and say
"This is no flattery"; these are counselors   10
That feelingly persuade me what I am.   11
Sweet are the uses of adversity,
Which, like the toad, ugly and venomous,   13
Wears yet a precious jewel in his head;
And this our life, exempt from public haunt,   15
Finds tongues in trees, books in the running brooks,
Sermons in stones, and good in everything.

AMIENS
I would not change it; happy is your grace
That can translate the stubbornness of fortune   19
Into so quiet and so sweet a style.   20

DUKE SENIOR
Come, shall we go and kill us venison?
And yet it irks me the poor dappled fools,   22
Being native burghers of this desert city,   23
Should, in their own confines, with forkèd heads   24
Have their round haunches gored.

FIRST LORD   Indeed, my lord,
The melancholy Jaques grieves at that,
And in that kind swears you do more usurp   27
Than doth your brother that hath banished you.

---

5 *penalty of Adam* (God expelled Adam, and Eve, from the perpetual warmth
and abundance of paradise as punishment for their transgression of eating
from the tree of knowledge; he thus subjected them to suffering, cold,
scrambling for scarce food, and, ultimately, disease and death; see Genesis 3)
6 *as* for example   7 *churlish* rough   11 *feelingly* through my senses   13–14
toad . . . head (toads were considered poisonous, but some thought that the
toad's head contained a jewel with various powers, including counteracting
the poison)   15 *exempt . . . haunt* (1) excluded from society, (2) banished
from the places where other people congregate   19 *stubbornness* hardness
22 *dappled* spotted; *fools* pitiable creatures   23 *burghers* citizens; *desert* uninhabited   24 *confines* territory; *forkèd heads* barbed arrowheads   27 *kind* way

	Today my Lord of Amiens and myself
30	Did steal behind him as he lay along
	Under an oak, whose antique root peeps out
32	Upon the brook that brawls along this wood,
33	To the which place a poor sequestered stag
	That from the hunter's aim had ta'en a hurt
	Did come to languish; and indeed, my lord,
	The wretched animal heaved forth such groans
37	That their discharge did stretch his leathern coat
38	Almost to bursting, and the big round tears
	Coursed one another down his innocent nose
40	In piteous chase; and thus the hairy fool,
41	Much markèd of the melancholy Jaques,
42	Stood on th' extremest verge of the swift brook,
	Augmenting it with tears.

DUKE SENIOR   But what said Jaques?

44   Did he not moralize this spectacle?

FIRST LORD

45   O, yes, into a thousand similes.

46   First, for his weeping into the needless stream:
       "Poor deer," quoth he, "thou mak'st a testament

48   As worldlings do, giving thy sum of more
       To that which had too much." Then, being there alone,

50   Left and abandoned of his velvet friend:
       "'Tis right," quoth he, "thus misery doth part

52   The flux of company." Anon a careless herd,
       Full of the pasture, jumps along by him
       And never stays to greet him; "Ay," quoth Jaques,

55   "Sweep on, you fat and greasy citizens,
       'Tis just the fashion; wherefore do you look

---

32 *brawls* babbles   33 *sequestered* separated from the rest of the herd   37 *leathern coat* skin   38 *tears* (wounded deer were commonly believed to shed tears)   40 *piteous* pitiable   41, 50 *of* by   42 *verge* bank   44 *moralize* draw a moral from   45 *similes* comparisons   46 *needless* needing no more water   48 *worldlings* mortals   50 *velvet* (1) the velvety texture of a deer's coat, (2) a fabric worn largely by high-status people, or *worldlings*   52 *flux* flood; *careless* carefree   55 *greasy* fattened up and ready for slaughter

Upon that poor and broken bankrupt there?"   57
Thus most invectively he pierceth through   58
The body of the country, city, court,
Yea, and of this our life, swearing that we   60
Are mere usurpers, tyrants, and what's worse,   61
To fright the animals and to kill them up   62
In their assigned and native dwelling place.   63

DUKE SENIOR
And did you leave him in this contemplation?

SECOND LORD
We did, my lord, weeping and commenting
Upon the sobbing deer.

DUKE SENIOR   Show me the place.
I love to cope him in these sullen fits,   67
For then he's full of matter.

FIRST LORD
I'll bring you to him straight.   *Exeunt.*

*

∾ **II.2** *Enter Duke [Frederick], with Lords.*

DUKE FREDERICK
Can it be possible that no man saw them?
It cannot be; some villains of my court
Are of consent and sufferance in this.   3

FIRST LORD
I cannot hear of any that did see her.
The ladies her attendants of her chamber
Saw her abed, and in the morning early
They found the bed untreasured of their mistress.   7

SECOND LORD
My lord, the roynish clown at whom so oft   8

---

57 *bankrupt* (1) bereft of companions, (2) unable to command sympathy or
help   58 *invectively* sharply   61 *what's worse* whatever could be worse   62
up off   63 *assigned* natural or God-given   67 *cope* grapple with
  II.2 Duke Frederick's palace   3 *of consent and sufferance* in connivance   7
untreasured emptied   8 *roynish* scurvy

    Your grace was wont to laugh is also missing.

10   Hisperia, the princess' gentlewoman,
    Confesses that she secretly o'erheard
    Your daughter and her cousin much commend

13   The parts and graces of the wrestler

14   That did but lately foil the sinewy Charles,
    And she believes, wherever they are gone,
    That youth is surely in their company.

DUKE FREDERICK
    Send to his brother, fetch that gallant hither;
    If he be absent, bring his brother to me;

19   I'll make him find him. Do this suddenly,

20   And let not search and inquisition quail
    To bring again these foolish runaways.   *Exeunt.*

*

∽ **II.3** *Enter Orlando and Adam.*

ORLANDO
    Who's there?

ADAM
    What, my young master, O my gentle master,

3   O my sweet master, O you memory
    Of old Sir Rowland, why, what make you here?
    Why are you virtuous? Why do people love you?
    And wherefore are you gentle, strong, and valiant?

7   Why would you be so fond to overcome

8   The bonny prizer of the humorous duke?
    Your praise is come too swiftly home before you.

10   Know you not, master, to some kind of men
    Their graces serve them but as enemies?

12   No more do yours. Your virtues, gentle master,

---

13 *parts* good qualities   14 *sinewy* muscular   19 *suddenly* at once   20 *inquisition quail* inquiry hesitate
    II.3 Before Oliver's house   3 *memory* living memorial   7 *fond* foolish
8 *bonny prizer* sturdy prizefighter; *humorous* moody   12 *No more* no better

Are sanctified and holy traitors to you.
O, what a world is this, when what is comely   14
Envenoms him that bears it!   15
[ORLANDO]
Why, what's the matter?
ADAM   O unhappy youth,
Come not within these doors; within this roof   17
The enemy of all your graces lives.
Your brother, no, no brother, yet the son
(Yet not the son, I will not call him son)   20
Of him I was about to call his father,
Hath heard your praises, and this night he means
To burn the lodging where you use to lie   23
And you within it. If he fail of that,
He will have other means to cut you off.
I overheard him, and his practices;   26
This is no place, this house is but a butchery;   27
Abhor it, fear it, do not enter it!
[ORLANDO]
Why, whither, Adam, wouldst thou have me go?
ADAM
No matter whither, so you come not here.   30
ORLANDO
What, wouldst thou have me go and beg my food,
Or with a base and boist'rous sword enforce   32
A thievish living on the common road?
This I must do, or know not what to do;
Yet this I will not do, do how I can.   35
I rather will subject me to the malice
Of a diverted blood and bloody brother.   37
ADAM
But do not so. I have five hundred crowns,

---

14 *comely* beautiful   15 *Envenoms* poisons   17 *within* under   23 *use* are accustomed   26 *practices* plots   27 *butchery* slaughterhouse   32 *boist'rous* violent   35 *do how ... can* whatever I do   37 *diverted* i.e., from natural affection; *bloody* bloodthirsty

39 The thrifty hire I saved under your father,
40 Which I did store to be my foster nurse
41 When service should in my old limbs lie lame
42 And unregarded age in corners thrown.
43 Take that, and he that doth the ravens feed,
Yea, providently caters for the sparrow,
Be comfort to my age. Here is the gold,
All this I give you. Let me be your servant;
47 Though I look old, yet I am strong and lusty,
For in my youth I never did apply
49 Hot and rebellious liquors in my blood,
50 Nor did not with unbashful forehead woo
The means of weakness and debility;
Therefore my age is as a lusty winter,
Frosty, but kindly. Let me go with you;
I'll do the service of a younger man
In all your business and necessities.

ORLANDO
O good old man, how well in thee appears
57 The constant service of the antique world,
58 When service sweat for duty, not for meed!
Thou art not for the fashion of these times,
60 Where none will sweat but for promotion,
61 And having that, do choke their service up
Even with the having; it is not so with thee.
But, poor old man, thou prun'st a rotten tree
That cannot so much as a blossom yield
65 In lieu of all thy pains and husbandry.
But come thy ways, we'll go along together,

---

39 *thrifty hire I saved* wages I thriftily saved   41 *service . . . lame* ability to serve should be weakened by old age   42 *unregarded* neglected, disrespected   43–44 *he . . . sparrow* i.e., God (see Job 38:41, Matthew 10:29, Luke 12:6, 12:24, Psalm 147:9)   47 *lusty* robust, vigorous   49 *rebellious* causing rebellion against self-control   50 *unbashful forehead* shameless face   57 *constant* faithful; *antique* ancient   58 *meed* reward   61–62 *do choke . . . having* cut their service off as soon as they gain promotion   65 *In lieu of* in return for; *husbandry* careful management

And ere we have thy youthful wages spent,
We'll light upon some settled low content.   68

ADAM

Master, go on, and I will follow thee
To the last gasp with truth and loyalty.   70
From seventeen years till now almost fourscore   71
Here livèd I, but now live here no more;
At seventeen years many their fortunes seek,
But at fourscore it is too late a week;   74
Yet fortune cannot recompense me better
Than to die well and not my master's debtor.   *Exeunt.*

*

∾ **II.4** *Enter Rosalind [dressed as] Ganymede, Celia
[dressed as] Aliena, and Touchstone.*

ROSALIND   O Jupiter, how merry are my spirits!   1

TOUCHSTONE   I care not for my spirits if my legs were
not weary.

ROSALIND   I could find in my heart to disgrace my man's
apparel and to cry like a woman; but I must comfort
the weaker vessel, as doublet and hose ought to show it-   6
self courageous to petticoat. Therefore, courage, good
Aliena!

CELIA   I pray you bear with me; I cannot go no further.

TOUCHSTONE   For my part, I had rather bear with you   10
than bear you; yet I should bear no cross if I did bear   11
you; for I think you have no money in your purse.

ROSALIND   Well, this is the Forest of Arden.

---

68 *low content* humble contentment   **71** *fourscore* four times twenty (i.e.,
eighty)   **74** *week* time

 II.4 The Forest of Arden   **1** *Jupiter* (another name for Jove, the king of
the gods in classical mythology, whom Ganymede serves); *merry* (perhaps
ironic, and often changed to "weary")   **6** *weaker vessel* (biblical term for
"wife" or "woman"; see 1 Peter 3:7); *doublet and hose* jacket and breeches
(men's clothes – i.e., manhood)   **11** *cross* (1) burden, (2) coin stamped with
a cross

TOUCHSTONE   Ay, now am I in Arden, the more fool I.
   When I was at home, I was in a better place, but travel-
   ers must be content.
      Enter Corin and Silvius.

ROSALIND
   Ay, be so, good Touchstone. Look you, who comes
      here,
   A young man and an old in solemn talk.

CORIN
   That is the way to make her scorn you still.

SILVIUS
20   O Corin, that thou knew'st how I do love her!

CORIN
   I partly guess, for I have loved ere now.

SILVIUS
   No, Corin, being old, thou canst not guess,
   Though in thy youth thou wast as true a lover
   As ever sighed upon a midnight pillow.
   But if thy love were ever like to mine,
   As sure I think did never man love so,
   How many actions most ridiculous
28   Hast thou been drawn to by thy fantasy?

CORIN
   Into a thousand that I have forgotten.

SILVIUS
30   O, thou didst then never love so heartily!
   If thou rememb'rest not the slightest folly
   That ever love did make thee run into,
   Thou hast not loved.
   Or if thou hast not sat as I do now,
   Wearying thy hearer in thy mistress' praise,
   Thou hast not loved.
   Or if thou hast not broke from company
   Abruptly, as my passion now makes me,
   Thou hast not loved.

---

28 *fantasy* imagination, desire

O Phebe, Phebe, Phebe!   *Exit.*   40
ROSALIND

Alas, poor shepherd! Searching of thy wound,   41
I have by hard adventure found mine own.

TOUCHSTONE   And I mine. I remember, when I was in
love I broke my sword upon a stone and bid him take   44
that for coming anight to Jane Smile; and I remember
the kissing of her batler, and the cow's dugs that her   46
pretty chapped hands had milked; and I remember the
wooing of a peasecod instead of her, from whom I took   48
two cods, and giving her them again, said with weeping
tears, "Wear these for my sake." We that are true lovers   50
run into strange capers; but as all is mortal in nature, so
is all nature in love mortal in folly.   52

ROSALIND   Thou speak'st wiser than thou art ware of.   53

TOUCHSTONE   Nay, I shall ne'er be ware of mine own wit
till I break my shins against it.

ROSALIND

Jove, Jove! this shepherd's passion
Is much upon my fashion.   57

TOUCHSTONE

And mine, but it grows something stale with me.   58

CELIA

I pray you, one of you question yond man
If he for gold will give us any food.   60
I faint almost to death.

TOUCHSTONE   Holla, you clown!   62

ROSALIND

Peace, fool! he's not thy kinsman.

---

41 *Searching* probing   44–45 *I broke . . . Jane Smile* (Touchstone treats the
stone as if it is his rival for Jane's affections)   46 *batler* (perhaps a bat used in
washing clothes)   48 *peasecod* peapod (considered a luck-bringing gift in
rural English courtship customs, perhaps because its phallic appearance associated it with fertility; "cod" and "peasecod" were both slang terms for the
male genitals)   52 *all . . . folly* i.e., all lovers reveal their humanity through
their foolishness   53 *ware* aware   57 *upon . . . fashion* like mine   58 *something* somewhat   62 *clown* bumpkin

CORIN Who calls?

TOUCHSTONE Your betters, sir.

CORIN Else are they very wretched.

ROSALIND
    Peace, I say! Good even to you, friend.

CORIN
    And to you, gentle sir, and to you all.

ROSALIND
    I prithee, shepherd, if that love or gold
70 Can in this desert place buy entertainment,
    Bring us where we may rest ourselves and feed.
    Here's a young maid with travel much oppressed,
73 And faints for succor.

CORIN   Fair sir, I pity her
    And wish, for her sake more than for mine own,
    My fortunes were more able to relieve her;
    But I am shepherd to another man
77 And do not shear the fleeces that I graze.
78 My master is of churlish disposition
79 And little recks to find the way to heaven
80 By doing deeds of hospitality.
81 Besides, his cote, his flocks, and bounds of feed
    Are now on sale, and at our sheepcote now,
    By reason of his absence, there is nothing
    That you will feed on; but what is, come see,
85 And in my voice most welcome shall you be.

ROSALIND
86 What is he that shall buy his flock and pasture?

CORIN
87 That young swain that you saw here but erewhile,
    That little cares for buying anything.

_____

70 *desert* uninhabited; *entertainment* food and lodging 73 *for succor* out of
need for food and rest 77 *shear . . . graze* i.e., I do not own the sheep I tend
and, therefore, I do not profit from the sale of their wool 78 *churlish* stingy
79 *recks* reckons 81 *cote* cottage; *bounds of feed* pastures 85 *in my voice* as
far as I have any influence 86 *What* who 87 *erewhile* a little while ago

ROSALIND
  I pray thee, if it stand with honesty,   89
  Buy thou the cottage, pasture, and the flock,   *90*
  And thou shalt have to pay for it of us.   91
CELIA
  And we will mend thy wages. I like this place   92
  And willingly could waste my time in it.   93
CORIN
  Assuredly the thing is to be sold.
  Go with me; if you like upon report   95
  The soil, the profit, and this kind of life,
  I will your very faithful feeder be   97
  And buy it with your gold right suddenly.   *Exeunt.*

*

❧ **II.5** *Enter Amiens, Jaques, and others.*

Song.

[AMIENS]
       Under the greenwood tree
        Who loves to lie with me,
      And turn his merry note   3
        Unto the sweet bird's throat,
    Come hither, come hither, come hither.
      Here shall he see no enemy
    But winter and rough weather.

JAQUES More, more, I prithee more!
AMIENS It will make you melancholy, Monsieur Jaques.
JAQUES I thank it. More, I prithee more! I can suck   *10*
melancholy out of a song as a weasel sucks eggs. More,
I prithee more!
AMIENS My voice is ragged. I know I cannot please you.

—————
89 *if . . . honesty* if it is consistent with honorable dealing 91 *have to pay*
have the money to pay 92 *mend* improve 93 *waste* spend 95 *report* further information 97 *feeder* servant
  II.5 The forest 3 *turn* attune

JAQUES   I do not desire you to please me; I do desire you
15   to sing. Come, more, another stanzo! Call you 'em
     stanzos?

AMIENS   What you will, Monsieur Jaques.

18   JAQUES   Nay, I care not for their names; they owe me
     nothing. Will you sing?

20   AMIENS   More at your request than to please myself.

JAQUES   Well then, if ever I thank any man, I'll thank
22   you. But that they call compliment is like th' encounter
23   of two dog apes, and when a man thanks me heartily,
     methinks I have given him a penny and he renders me
25   the beggarly thanks. Come, sing; and you that will not,
     hold your tongues.

27   AMIENS   Well, I'll end the song. Sirs, cover the while; the
     duke will drink under this tree. He hath been all this
29   day to look you.

30   JAQUES   And I have been all this day to avoid him. He is
31   too disputable for my company. I think of as many
     matters as he, but I give heaven thanks and make no
     boast of them. Come, warble, come.

Song.

All together here.
          Who doth ambition shun
              And loves to live i' th' sun,
          Seeking the food he eats,
              And pleased with what he gets,
          Come hither, come hither, come hither.
              Here shall he see no enemy
40   But winter and rough weather.

---

15 *stanzo* stanza or verse   18–19 *names . . . nothing* i.e., I'd care about their
names only if they owed me money   22 *compliment* politeness   22–23 *th'
encounter . . . dog apes* i.e., mutual back-scratching or insincere politeness
23 *dog apes* baboons   25 *beggarly* effusive, like a beggar's   27 *cover the while*
meanwhile, set the table   29 *to look* looking for   31 *disputable* argumenta-
tive

JAQUES   I'll give you a verse to this note that I made yes-   41
terday in despite of my invention.   42

AMIENS   And I'll sing it.

JAQUES   Thus it goes.

[Gives a paper.]

AMIENS

       If it do come to pass   45
       That any man turn ass,
       Leaving his wealth and ease
       A stubborn will to please,
       Ducdame, ducdame, ducdame.   49
       Here shall he see gross fools as he,   50
       An if he will come to me.   51

What's that "ducdame"?

JAQUES   'Tis a Greek invocation to call fools into a circle.
I'll go sleep, if I can; if I cannot, I'll rail against all the
first-born of Egypt.   55

AMIENS   And I'll go seek the duke. His banquet is prepared.   *Exeunt.*

*

∾ **II.6** *Enter Orlando and Adam.*

ADAM   Dear master, I can go no further. O, I die for
food. Here lie I down and measure out my grave.
Farewell, kind master.

ORLANDO   Why, how now, Adam? no greater heart in
thee? Live a little, comfort a little, cheer thyself a little. If

---

41 *note* tune   42 *in . . . invention* although I lack imagination   45 s.p.
(many editions assign this song to Jaques)   49 *Ducdame* (probably a non-
sense word, pronounced as three syllables)   51 *An if* if   55 *first-born of
Egypt* (In the Old Testament, God caused the deaths of all of the Egyptian
first-born, to punish Pharaoh for preventing the Israelites from leaving
Egypt; see Exodus 12. In this play, Orlando rails against his "first-born"
brother, and Duke Frederick usurps the dukedom from his.)
   II.6 The forest

6   this uncouth forest yield anything savage, I will either be
7   food for it or bring it for food to thee. Thy conceit is
8   nearer death than thy powers. For my sake be comfort-
9   able; hold death awhile at the arm's end. I will here be
10 with thee presently, and if I bring thee not something to
    eat, I will give thee leave to die; but if thou diest before I
12 come, thou art a mocker of my labor. Well said; thou
13 lookest cheerly, and I'll be with thee quickly. Yet thou
    liest in the bleak air. Come, I will bear thee to some shel-
    ter, and thou shalt not die for lack of a dinner if there live
    anything in this desert. Cheerly, good Adam.   *Exeunt.*

                              *

⁓ **II.7** *Enter Duke Senior, and Lords, [dressed] like Outlaws.*

DUKE SENIOR
    I think he be transformed into a beast,
2   For I can nowhere find him like a man.

FIRST LORD
    My lord, he is but even now gone hence;
    Here was he merry, hearing of a song.

DUKE SENIOR
5   If he, compact of jars, grow musical,
6   We shall have shortly discord in the spheres.
    Go seek him; tell him I would speak with him.
        Enter Jaques.

FIRST LORD
    He saves my labor by his own approach.

_____

6 *uncouth* uncivilized   7 *conceit* imagination   8 *powers* body   8–9 *comfort-able* cheerful   9 *end* length   10 *presently* immediately   12 *said* done   13 *cheerly* cheerfully

II.7 Duke Senior's camp in the forest   2 *like* in the shape of   5 *compact of jars* composed of discords   6 *spheres* (alluding to a popular theory, attributed to Pythagoras, according to which the earth stood at the center of a series of transparent spheres; as these spheres moved, they produced harmonious music inaudible to humans)

DUKE SENIOR
　　Why, how now, monsieur, what a life is this,
　　That your poor friends must woo your company?　　*10*
　　What, you look merrily.
JAQUES
　　A fool, a fool! I met a fool i' th' forest,
　　A motley fool! a miserable world!　　*13*
　　As I do live by food, I met a fool
　　Who laid him down and basked him in the sun
　　And railed on Lady Fortune in good terms,
　　In good set terms, and yet a motley fool.　　*17*
　　"Good morrow, fool," quoth I. "No, sir," quoth he,
　　"Call me not fool till heaven hath sent me fortune."
　　And then he drew a dial from his poke,　　*20*
　　And looking on it with lackluster eye,
　　Says very wisely, "It is ten o'clock.
　　Thus we may see," quoth he, "how the world wags.
　　'Tis but an hour ago since it was nine,
　　And after one hour more 'twill be eleven;
　　And so, from hour to hour, we ripe and ripe,　　*26*
　　And then, from hour to hour, we rot and rot;　　*27*
　　And thereby hangs a tale." When I did hear
　　The motley fool thus moral on the time,　　*29*
　　My lungs began to crow like chanticleer　　*30*
　　That fools should be so deep contemplative;
　　And I did laugh sans intermission　　*32*
　　An hour by his dial. O noble fool,
　　A worthy fool! Motley's the only wear.　　*34*

---

13 *motley* wearing a costume of mixed colors, the conventional dress of a professional jester   17 *set* conventional or well-practiced   20 *dial* portable sundial; *poke* pocket   26–28 *from hour . . . tale* (the homonyms and puns here associate men's maturation and mortality with sex and disease: *hour* sounds like and suggests "whore"; *tale* sounds like and suggests "tail" or penis)   26 *ripe* mature sexually   27 *rot* decay (with a suggestion of disease transmitted through "rutting" or sexual intercourse)   29 *moral* moralize   30 *crow like chanticleer* exclaim triumphantly, like a crowing cock   32 *sans* without   34 *wear* costume

DUKE SENIOR
What fool is this?

JAQUES
O worthy fool! One that hath been a courtier,
And says, if ladies be but young and fair,
They have the gift to know it. And in his brain,
39 Which is as dry as the remainder biscuit
40 After a voyage, he hath strange places crammed
41 With observation, the which he vents
In mangled forms. O that I were a fool!
I am ambitious for a motley coat.

DUKE SENIOR
44 Thou shalt have one.

JAQUES   It is my only suit,
Provided that you weed your better judgments
46 Of all opinion that grows rank in them
That I am wise. I must have liberty
48 Withal, as large a charter as the wind,
To blow on whom I please, for so fools have.
50 And they that are most gallèd with my folly,
They most must laugh. And why, sir, must they so?
The why is plain as way to parish church:
He that a fool doth very wisely hit
Doth very foolishly, although he smart,
55 Not to seem senseless of the bob. If not,
56 The wise man's folly is anatomized
57 Even by the squand'ring glances of the fool.
58 Invest me in my motley, give me leave
To speak my mind, and I will through and through
60 Cleanse the foul body of th' infected world,
If they will patiently receive my medicine.

---

39 *dry* (a dry brain was supposedly retentive); *remainder* leftover 40 *places* (in his brain) 41 *vents* expresses 44 *suit* (1) costume, (2) request 46 *rank* wild 48 W*ithal* (along with my suit of motley); *large a charter* broad license 50 *gallèd* rubbed on a sore spot 55 *Not . . . senseless* not to ignore; *bob* jab 56 *anatomized* revealed, as by dissection 57 *squandering glances* random hits 58 *Invest* dress

DUKE SENIOR
  Fie on thee! I can tell what thou wouldst do.

JAQUES
  What, for a counter, would I do but good?   63

DUKE SENIOR
  Most mischievous foul sin, in chiding sin.
  For thou thyself hast been a libertine,
  As sensual as the brutish sting itself;   66
  And all th' embossèd sores and headed evils   67
  That thou with license of free foot hast caught,   68
  Wouldst thou disgorge into the general world.

JAQUES
  Why, who cries out on pride   70
  That can therein tax any private party?   71
  Doth it not flow as hugely as the sea
  Till that the weary very means do ebb?   73
  What woman in the city do I name
  When that I say the city woman bears
  The cost of princes on unworthy shoulders?   76
  Who can come in and say that I mean her,
  When such a one as she, such is her neighbor?
  Or what is he of basest function   79
  That says his bravery is not on my cost,   80
  Thinking that I mean him, but therein suits   81
  His folly to the mettle of my speech?
  There then, how then, what then? Let me see wherein
  My tongue hath wronged him. If it do him right, 84
  Then he hath wronged himself. If he be free,   85

---

63 *counter* worthless coin 66 *brutish sting* carnal appetite 67 *embossèd* swollen; *headed evils* evils or diseases that have come to a head, like boils (Duke Senior describes Jaques as having been contaminated by his self-indulgence, perhaps in the form of a sexually transmitted disease) 68 *license . . . foot* freedom to roam (including sexually) 71 *tax* censure 73 *very means* source itself (i.e., pride exhausts itself) 76 *cost* costly clothes 79 *function* position in society 80 *says . . . cost* says his finery is not bought at my price (i.e., denies my criticism) 81–82 *therein . . . speech* thus matches his folly with the substance of my remarks 84 *do . . . right* describes him accurately 85 *free* i.e., from blame

Why, then my taxing like a wild goose flies
Unclaimed of any man. But who comes here?
Enter Orlando [with his sword drawn].

ORLANDO
Forbear, and eat no more!

JAQUES   Why, I have eat none yet.

ORLANDO
Nor shalt not, till necessity be served.

JAQUES
90   Of what kind should this cock come of?

DUKE SENIOR
Art thou thus boldened, man, by thy distress,
Or else a rude despiser of good manners,
93   That in civility thou seem'st so empty?

ORLANDO
94   You touched my vein at first. The thorny point
95   Of bare distress hath ta'en from me the show
96   Of smooth civility; yet am I inland bred
97   And know some nurture. But forbear, I say!
He dies that touches any of this fruit
99   Till I and my affairs are answerèd.

JAQUES
100   An you will not be answered with reason, I must die.

DUKE SENIOR
101   What would you have? Your gentleness shall force
More than your force move us to gentleness.

ORLANDO
I almost die for food, and let me have it!

DUKE SENIOR
Sit down and feed, and welcome to our table.

---

90 *Of... of* i.e., what kind of fighting *cock* or troublemaker is this   93
empty lacking   94 *vein* disposition   95 *show* performance   96 *inland bred*
raised in civilized society   97 *nurture* proper upbringing   99 *answerèd* given
attention   100 *An* if; *reason* (perhaps a pun on "raisin" – i.e., grape)   101
gentleness (1) gentle birth or status, (2) conduct befitting one of such status,
(3) kindness, civility (Orlando and the duke play on the multiple meanings
of this word)

ORLANDO
  Speak you so gently? Pardon me, I pray you.
  I thought that all things had been savage here,
  And therefore put I on the countenance   107
  Of stern commandment. But whate'er you are
  That in this desert inaccessible,
  Under the shade of melancholy boughs,   110
  Lose and neglect the creeping hours of time;
  If ever you have looked on better days,
  If ever been where bells have knolled to church,   113
  If ever sat at any good man's feast,
  If ever from your eyelids wiped a tear
  And know what 'tis to pity and be pitied,
  Let gentleness my strong enforcement be;   117
  In the which hope I blush, and hide my sword.   118

DUKE SENIOR
  True is it that we have seen better days,
  And have with holy bell been knolled to church,   120
  And sat at good men's feasts, and wiped our eyes
  Of drops that sacred pity hath engendered;
  And therefore sit you down in gentleness,
  And take upon command what help we have   124
  That to your wanting may be ministered.   125

ORLANDO
  Then but forbear your food a little while,
  Whiles, like a doe, I go to find my fawn
  And give it food. There is an old poor man
  Who after me hath many a weary step
  Limped in pure love. Till he be first sufficed,   130
  Oppressed with two weak evils, age and hunger,
  I will not touch a bit.

DUKE SENIOR   Go find him out,
  And we will nothing waste till you return.

---

107 *countenance* appearance 113 *knolled* called by chimes 117 *enforce-ment* inducement 118 *hide* sheathe 124 *upon command* for the asking
125 *wanting* need 130 *sufficed* satisfied

ORLANDO
 I thank ye, and be blessed for your good comfort! *[Exit.]*
DUKE SENIOR
135 Thou seest we are not all alone unhappy:
     This wide and universal theater
     Presents more woeful pageants than the scene
138 Wherein we play in.
       JAQUES   All the world's a stage,
     And all the men and women merely players;
140 They have their exits and their entrances,
     And one man in his time plays many parts,
     His acts being seven ages. At first, the infant,
143 Mewling and puking in the nurse's arms.
     Then the whining schoolboy, with his satchel
     And shining morning face, creeping like snail
     Unwillingly to school. And then the lover,
     Sighing like furnace, with a woeful ballad
     Made to his mistress' eyebrow. Then a soldier,
149 Full of strange oaths and bearded like the pard,
150 Jealous in honor, sudden and quick in quarrel,
     Seeking the bubble reputation
152 Even in the cannon's mouth. And then the justice,
153 In fair round belly with good capon lined,
     With eyes severe and beard of formal cut,
155 Full of wise saws and modern instances;
     And so he plays his part. The sixth age shifts
157 Into the lean and slippered pantaloon,
158 With spectacles on nose and pouch on side;

---

135 *all . . . unhappy* the only ones suffering 138 *All . . . stage* (a stock metaphor in classical and Renaissance literature) 143 *Mewling* crying; *nurse* wet nurse (a woman paid to breast-feed an infant) 149 *pard* leopard 150 *Jealous in* on the alert for possible slights to; *sudden* rash 152 *justice* justice of the peace, judge 153 *capon* (alluding to the well-known Elizabethan practice of offering a gift of a capon to a judge, in hope of gaining his favor) 155 *saws* sayings; *modern instances* everyday examples 157 *pantaloon* ridiculous old man (a stock figure in commedia dell'arte, or Italian comedy) 158 *pouch* purse

His youthful hose, well saved, a world too wide   159
For his shrunk shank, and his big manly voice,   *160*
Turning again toward childish treble, pipes
And whistles in his sound. Last scene of all,   162
That ends this strange eventful history,
Is second childishness and mere oblivion,
Sans teeth, sans eyes, sans taste, sans everything.   165
    Enter Orlando, with Adam.

DUKE SENIOR
  Welcome. Set down your venerable burden
  And let him feed.

ORLANDO
  I thank you most for him.

ADAM   So had you need.
  I scarce can speak to thank you for myself.

DUKE SENIOR
  Welcome, fall to. I will not trouble you   *170*
  As yet to question you about your fortunes.
  Give us some music; and, good cousin, sing.

Song.

[AMIENS]
    Blow, blow, thou winter wind,
    Thou art not so unkind
      As man's ingratitude:
    Thy tooth is not so keen,
    Because thou art not seen,
      Although thy breath be rude.
  Heigh-ho, sing heigh-ho, unto the green holly.
  Most friendship is faining, most loving mere folly: *180*
    Then, heigh-ho, the holly.
    This life is most jolly.

    Freeze, freeze, thou bitter sky
    That dost not bite so nigh   184

---

159 *youthful hose* breeches he has had since he was young 162 *his* its 165 *sans* without 184 *nigh* closely

As benefits forgot:
186   Though thou the waters warp,
         Thy sting is not so sharp
         As friend remembered not.
    Heigh-ho, sing, etc.

DUKE SENIOR
190   If that you were the good Sir Rowland's son,
      As you have whispered faithfully you were,
192   And as mine eye doth his effigies witness
193   Most truly limned and living in your face,
      Be truly welcome hither. I am the duke
195   That loved your father. The residue of your fortune
      Go to my cave and tell me. Good old man,
      Thou art right welcome, as thy master is.
      Support him by the arm. Give me your hand,
      And let me all your fortunes understand.   *Exeunt.*

                          *

❧ III.1 *Enter Duke [Frederick], Lords, and Oliver.*

DUKE FREDERICK
      Not see him since? Sir, sir, that cannot be.
2   But were I not the better part made mercy,
3   I should not seek an absent argument
4   Of my revenge, thou present. But look to it:
      Find out thy brother, wheresoe'er he is;
6   Seek him with candle; bring him dead or living
7   Within this twelvemonth, or turn thou no more
8   To seek a living in our territory.
      Thy lands, and all things that thou dost call thine
10   Worth seizure, do we seize into our hands

───────────

186 *warp* freeze 192 *effigies* likeness 193 *limned* portrayed 195
residue . . . fortune the rest of what has happened to you
    III.1 Within Duke Frederick's palace 2 *better . . . mercy* more merciful
than not 3 *argument* subject (i.e., Orlando) 4 *thou present* you being present 6 *with candle* tirelessly, thoroughly 7 *turn* return 8 *a living* your life

Till thou canst quit thee by thy brother's mouth   11
Of what we think against thee.

OLIVER
O that your highness knew my heart in this!
I never loved my brother in my life.

DUKE FREDERICK
More villain thou. Well, push him out of doors,
And let my officers of such a nature   16
Make an extent upon his house and lands.   17
Do this expediently and turn him going.   *Exeunt.*   18

*

∾ **III.2** *Enter Orlando [with a paper].*

ORLANDO
Hang there, my verse, in witness of my love;
    And thou, thrice-crownèd Queen of Night, survey   2
With thy chaste eye, from thy pale sphere above,
    Thy huntress' name that my full life doth sway.   4
O Rosalind! these trees shall be my books,
    And in their barks my thoughts I'll character,   6
That every eye which in this forest looks
    Shall see thy virtue witnessed everywhere.   8
Run, run, Orlando, carve on every tree
The fair, the chaste, and unexpressive she.   *Exit.*   10
    Enter Corin and [Touchstone the] Clown.
CORIN   And how like you this shepherd's life, Master
Touchstone?

---

11 *quit* acquit   16 *of . . . nature* whose job it is   17 *Make . . . upon* (1) seize
by writ, (2) make an inventory of   18 *turn . . . going* kick him out
    III.2 The Forest of Arden   2 *thrice-crownèd . . . Night* the moon (the
triple crowning probably refers to the three goddesses associated with the
night at the three different levels of the cosmos: Proserpina [the under-
world], Diana [the earth], and Cynthia, also known as Phoebe or Luna [the
heavens])   4 *Thy huntress' name* (Orlando imagines Rosalind as a chaste
huntress waiting on Diana); *my . . . sway* rules over my whole life   6 *charac-*
ter inscribe   8 *virtue* excellence   10 *unexpressive* beyond expression

13 TOUCHSTONE Truly, shepherd, in respect of itself, it is a
    good life; but in respect that it is a shepherd's life, it is
15 naught. In respect that it is solitary, I like it very well;
16 but in respect that it is private, it is a very vile life. Now
    in respect it is in the fields, it pleaseth me well; but in
18 respect it is not in the court, it is tedious. As it is a spare
19 life, look you, it fits my humor well; but as there is no
20 more plenty in it, it goes much against my stomach.
    Hast any philosophy in thee, shepherd?
    CORIN No more but that I know the more one sickens
    the worse at ease he is; and that he that wants money,
    means, and content is without three good friends; that
    the property of rain is to wet and fire to burn; that good
    pasture makes fat sheep, and that a great cause of the
    night is lack of the sun; that he that hath learned no wit
28 by nature nor art may complain of good breeding, or
    comes of a very dull kindred.
30 TOUCHSTONE Such a one is a natural philosopher. Wast
    ever in court, shepherd?
    CORIN No, truly.
    TOUCHSTONE Then thou art damned.
34 CORIN Nay, I hope.
    TOUCHSTONE Truly thou art damned, like an ill-roasted
    egg, all on one side.
    CORIN For not being at court? Your reason.
    TOUCHSTONE Why, if thou never wast at court, thou
    never sawest good manners; if thou never sawest good
40 manners, then thy manners must be wicked; and
    wickedness is sin, and sin is damnation. Thou art in a
42 parlous state, shepherd.
    CORIN Not a whit, Touchstone. Those that are good
    manners at the court are as ridiculous in the country as

---

13 *in respect of* considering 15 *naught* bad (with a pun on "nought," worthless) 16 *private* lonely 18 *spare* meager 19 *humor* state of mind 20
stomach taste, preference 28 *complain of* lament the lack of 34 *Nay, I hope*
i.e., I have hope of salvation 40 *manners* (1) polite conduct, (2) morals 42
parlous perilous (a dialectal form)

the behavior of the country is most mockable at the
court. You told me you salute not at the court but you   46
kiss your hands. That courtesy would be uncleanly if
courtiers were shepherds.

TOUCHSTONE   Instance, briefly; come, instance.   49

CORIN   Why, we are still handling our ewes, and their   50
fells you know are greasy.   51

TOUCHSTONE   Why, do not your courtier's hands sweat?
and is not the grease of a mutton as wholesome as the
sweat of a man? Shallow, shallow. A better instance, I
say; come.

CORIN   Besides, our hands are hard.

TOUCHSTONE   Your lips will feel them the sooner. Shallow again. A more sounder instance, come.

CORIN   And they are often tarred over with the surgery   59
of our sheep, and would you have us kiss tar? The   60
courtier's hands are perfumed with civet.   61

TOUCHSTONE   Most shallow man! Thou worms' meat in   62
respect of a good piece of flesh indeed! Learn of the
wise, and perpend. Civet is of a baser birth than tar, the   64
very uncleanly flux of a cat. Mend the instance, shep-   65
herd.

CORIN   You have too courtly a wit for me; I'll rest.

TOUCHSTONE   Wilt thou rest damned? God help thee,
shallow man! God make incision in thee! thou art raw.   69

CORIN   Sir, I am a true laborer; I earn that I eat, get that   70
I wear, owe no man hate, envy no man's happiness, glad
of other men's good, content with my harm; and the   72

---

46 *salute* greet one another; *but* unless   49 *Instance* proof   50 *still* continu-
ally   51 *fells* fleeces   59 *tarred . . . surgery* covered with the tar used as oint-
ment for sores   61 *civet* a musky scented substance used as an ingredient in
perfumes, squeezed from the anal glands of the civet cat   62–63 *worms'*
meat . . . of food for worms or rotting flesh in comparison to   64 *perpend*
consider   65 *flux* secretion   69 *make incision in* i.e., (1) cut you to draw
blood as a cure for disease, (2) tenderize you as one would a cheap, tough cut
of meat; *raw* (1) crude, unfinished, (2) sore, requiring medical help   72 *harm*
bad luck

greatest of my pride is to see my ewes graze and my lambs suck.

TOUCHSTONE That is another simple sin in you: to bring the ewes and the rams together and to offer to get
77 your living by the copulation of cattle, to be bawd to a
78 bellwether and to betray a she-lamb of a twelvemonth
79 to a crookèd-pated old cuckoldly ram, out of all reason-
80 able match. If thou beest not damned for this, the devil himself will have no shepherds; I cannot see else how thou shouldst scape.

CORIN Here comes young Master Ganymede, my new mistress's brother.

Enter Rosalind [dressed as Ganymede with a paper].

ROSALIND *[Reads.]*
85 "From the east to western Ind,
No jewel is like Rosalind.
Her worth, being mounted on the wind,
Through all the world bears Rosalind.
89 All the pictures fairest lined
90 Are but black to Rosalind.
Let no face be kept in mind
But the fair of Rosalind."

TOUCHSTONE I'll rhyme you so eight years together,
94 dinners and suppers and sleeping hours excepted. It is the right butterwomen's rank to market.

ROSALIND Out, fool!

TOUCHSTONE For a taste:

---

77 *bawd* sexual procurer or pimp 78 *bellwether* leading sheep of the flock, usually adorned with a bell 79 *crookèd-pated* with crooked horns; *cuckoldly* i.e., because he has horns or because he puts horns on others (the cuckold, or man whose wife cheated on him, was popularly imagined as sprouting horns) 79–80 *out . . . match* outside the realm of acceptable matings 80–81 *devil . . . shepherds* it is because the devil wants no shepherds in hell 85–92 *From . . . Rosalind* (the last word in each line is pronounced with a long *i* and a sounded *d*) 89 *lined* outlined, drawn 94–95 *It is . . . market* i.e., the verses jog on monotonously like farm women riding to market, or they are full of hot air, like women chatting on their way to market

If a hart do lack a hind,
Let him seek out Rosalind.
If the cat will after kind,   *100*
So be sure will Rosalind.
Wintered garments must be lined,   *102*
So must slender Rosalind.
They that reap must sheaf and bind,
Then to cart with Rosalind.   *105*
Sweetest nut hath sourest rind,
Such a nut is Rosalind.
He that sweetest rose will find
Must find love's prick, and Rosalind.   *109*

This is the very false gallop of verses. Why do you in-   *110*
fect yourself with them?

ROSALIND   Peace, you dull fool! I found them on a tree.

TOUCHSTONE   Truly the tree yields bad fruit.

ROSALIND   I'll graft it with you and then I shall graft it   *114*
with a medlar. Then it will be the earliest fruit i' th'   *115*
country; for you'll be rotten ere you be half ripe, and
that's the right virtue of the medlar.

TOUCHSTONE   You have said; but whether wisely or no,
let the forest judge.

Enter Celia [dressed as Aliena] with a [paper].

ROSALIND   Peace! Here comes my sister reading; stand   *120*
aside.

CELIA

"Why should this a desert be?
For it is unpeopled? No.

---

102 *Wintered* prepared for winter; *lined* (1) filled with a heavier inner layer,
(2) mated (usually used with reference to a female dog)   105 *to cart* (1) as
harvests were loaded on a cart to be taken to market, (2) as women convicted
of prostitution or other transgressions were drawn through the streets on a
cart, exposed to scrutiny and abuse (sometimes such women were stripped to
the waist and whipped)   109 *prick* (1) thorn, (2) penis   110 *false* defective;
gallop meter (i.e., the verses get off on the wrong foot, cantering unevenly)
114 *you* (there may be a pun here on "yew")   115 *medlar* a kind of pear not
ready to eat until it starts to decay (with a pun on "meddler")

Tongues I'll hang on every tree
125   That shall civil sayings show:
Some, how brief the life of man
127   Runs his erring pilgrimage,
128   That the stretching of a span
129   Buckles in his sum of age;
130   Some, of violated vows
'Twixt the souls of friend and friend;
But upon the fairest boughs,
Or at every sentence end,
Will I 'Rosalinda' write,
Teaching all that read to know
136   The quintessence of every sprite
137   Heaven would in little show.
Therefore heaven Nature charged
That one body should be filled
140   With all graces wide-enlarged.
Nature presently distilled
142   Helen's cheek, but not her heart,
143   Cleopatra's majesty,
144   Atalanta's better part,
145   Sad Lucretia's modesty.
Thus Rosalind of many parts

---

125 *civil sayings* civilized comments   **127** *erring* wandering   **128** *stretching of a span* breadth of an open hand   **129** *Buckles in* encompasses; *sum of age* lifetime   **136** *quintessence* pure essence (accent on the first syllable); *sprite* spirit   **137** *in little* i.e., in one person, in miniature   **140** *With . . . enlarged* (graces that are usually spread across many people are concentrated in Rosalind)   **142** *cheek* beauty; *heart* i.e., false heart (In Homer's *Iliad,* Paris's abduction of Helen of Troy from her husband, Menelaus, instigates the Trojan War. Some versions depict Helen not as a victim of abduction but as a traitor, both to her husband and to Troy.)   **143** *Cleopatra* a queen of Egypt (see Shakespeare's *Antony and Cleopatra*)   **144** *Atalanta* (In Greek mythology, Atalanta challenged her suitors to a race. She was winning until one of them threw golden apples into her path. When she stopped to pick them up, she lost her lead. Thus her greed defeated her *better part* – i.e., her speed or beauty.)   **145** *Sad* serious; *Lucretia* a Roman matron who killed herself after she had been raped by the tyrant Tarquin (see Shakespeare's *Lucrece*)

By heavenly synod was devised,   147
Of many faces, eyes, and hearts,
    To have the touches dearest prized.   149
Heaven would that she these gifts should have,   *150*
And I to live and die her slave."

ROSALIND   O most gentle Jupiter, what tedious homily
of love have you wearied your parishioners withal, and
never cried, "Have patience, good people"!

CELIA   How now? Back, friends. Shepherd, go off a little.
Go with him, sirrah.

TOUCHSTONE   Come, shepherd, let us make an honorable retreat; though not with bag and baggage, yet with   158
scrip and scrippage.   *Exit [with Corin].*

CELIA   Didst thou hear these verses?   *160*

ROSALIND   O, yes, I heard them all, and more too; for
some of them had in them more feet than the verses   162
would bear.

CELIA   That's no matter. The feet might bear the verses. 164

ROSALIND   Ay, but the feet were lame, and could not   165
bear themselves without the verse, and therefore stood
lamely in the verse.

CELIA   But didst thou hear without wondering how thy
name should be hanged and carved upon these trees?

ROSALIND   I was seven of the nine days out of the won-   170
der before you came; for look here what I found on a
palm tree. I was never so berhymed since Pythagoras'   172
time that I was an Irish rat, which I can hardly re-   173
member.

---

147 *synod* assembly   149 *touches* features   158–59 *not . . . scrippage* i.e., not
like an army in retreat with all of its equipment but as a shepherd with his
pouch (*scrip*) and its contents   162 *feet* (in the following lines, Rosalind
plays on the meaning of feet as divisions of verse)   164 *bear* (1) allow, (2)
carry   165 *lame* (1) crippled, (2) bad   170 *nine days* (a reference to the
common expression "a nine days' wonder," which suggests that even the
most sensational occurrence provokes wonder for only nine days)   172
berhymed rhymed about; *Pythagoras* (to whom was attributed the doctrine of
transmigration of souls)   173 *Irish rat* (alluding to the belief that Irish sor-
cerers could kill animals by means of rhymed spells)

175 CELIA Trow you who hath done this?

  ROSALIND Is it a man?

177 CELIA And a chain that you once wore, about his neck.
  Change you color?

  ROSALIND I prithee who?

180 CELIA O Lord, Lord, it is a hard matter for friends to
181 meet; but mountains may be removed with earth-
182 quakes, and so encounter.

  ROSALIND Nay, but who is it?

  CELIA Is it possible?

185 ROSALIND Nay, I prithee now with most petitionary ve-
  hemence, tell me who it is.

  CELIA O wonderful, wonderful, and most wonderful
188 wonderful, and yet again wonderful, and after that, out
  of all hooping!

190 ROSALIND Good my complexion! Dost thou think,
191 though I am caparisoned like a man, I have a doublet
192 and hose in my disposition? One inch of delay more is
  a South Sea of discovery. I prithee tell me who is it
  quickly, and speak apace. I would thou couldst stam-
  mer, that thou mightst pour this concealed man out of
  thy mouth as wine comes out of a narrow-mouthed
  bottle; either too much at once, or none at all. I prithee
  take the cork out of thy mouth, that I may drink thy
  tidings.

200 CELIA So you may put a man in your belly.

201 ROSALIND Is he of God's making? What manner of man?
  Is his head worth a hat? or his chin worth a beard?

  CELIA Nay, he hath but a little beard.

---

175 *Trow you* have you any idea   177 *chain* (see I.2.232 s.d.)   181 *removed with* moved by   182 *encounter* be brought together   185 *petitionary* suppli-ant   188–89 *out of all hooping* beyond all measure   190 *Good my complex-ion* O my (feminine) temperament   191 *caparisoned* bedecked   192–93 *One . . . discovery* another minute of waiting will be as endless as a journey of exploration to the South Seas   200 *belly* (1) stomach, (2) womb   201 *of God's making* i.e., a real man, of flesh and blood

ROSALIND   Why, God will send more, if the man will be
thankful. Let me stay the growth of his beard, if thou   205
delay me not the knowledge of his chin.

CELIA   It is young Orlando, that tripped up the wrestler's
heels and your heart both in an instant.

ROSALIND   Nay, but the devil take mocking! Speak sad   209
brow and true maid.   *210*

CELIA   I' faith, coz, 'tis he.

ROSALIND   Orlando?

CELIA   Orlando.

ROSALIND   Alas the day! what shall I do with my doublet
and hose? What did he when thou sawest him? What
said he? How looked he? Wherein went he? What   216
makes he here? Did he ask for me? Where remains he?   217
How parted he with thee? and when shalt thou see him
again? Answer me in one word.

CELIA   You must borrow me Gargantua's mouth first; 'tis   220
a word too great for any mouth of this age's size. To say
ay and no to these particulars is more than to answer in
a catechism.   223

ROSALIND   But doth he know that I am in this forest,
and in man's apparel? Looks he as freshly as he did the   225
day he wrestled?

CELIA   It is as easy to count atomies as to resolve the   227
propositions of a lover; but take a taste of my finding
him, and relish it with good observance. I found him   229
under a tree, like a dropped acorn.   *230*

ROSALIND   It may well be called Jove's tree when it drops   231
forth such fruit.

------

205 *stay* wait for   209–10 *sad . . . maid* seriously and truthfully   216
Wherein went he what did he wear   217 *makes* does   220 *Gargantua* a giant
in French folklore who, in Rabelais's famous version of the story, swallowed
five pilgrims in a salad   223 *catechism* a series of standard questions and
memorized answers used to teach the fundamentals of church doctrine   225
freshly robust   227 *atomies* motes   227–28 *resolve the propositions* answer
the questions   229 *relish it* heighten it with sauce; *observance* attention
231 *Jove's tree* (the oak was sacred to Jove)

CELIA   Give me audience, good madam.

ROSALIND   Proceed.

CELIA   There lay he stretched along like a wounded knight.

ROSALIND   Though it be pity to see such a sight, it well becomes the ground.

239 CELIA   Cry "holla" to thy tongue, I prithee; it curvets un-
240 seasonably. He was furnished like a hunter.

ROSALIND   O, ominous! he comes to kill my heart.

242 CELIA   I would sing my song without a burden. Thou
243 bringest me out of tune.

ROSALIND   Do you not know I am a woman? When I think, I must speak. Sweet, say on.

Enter Orlando and Jaques.

CELIA   You bring me out. Soft. Comes he not here?

ROSALIND   'Tis he! Slink by, and note him.

JAQUES   I thank you for your company; but, good faith, I
249 had as lief have been myself alone.

250 ORLANDO   And so had I; but yet for fashion sake I thank you too for your society.

252 JAQUES   God b' wi' you; let's meet as little as we can.

ORLANDO   I do desire we may be better strangers.

JAQUES   I pray you mar no more trees with writing love songs in their barks.

ORLANDO   I pray you mar no more of my verses with
257 reading them ill-favoredly.

JAQUES   Rosalind is your love's name?

ORLANDO   Yes, just.

260 JAQUES   I do not like her name.

ORLANDO   There was no thought of pleasing you when she was christened.

JAQUES   What stature is she of?

---

239 *holla* halt; *curvets* prances   240 *furnished* outfitted   242 *burden* under-
song, refrain   243 *bringest me out* throw me off tune   249 *as lief* just as
soon   250 *fashion* appearances'   252 *Gòd b' wi' you* good-bye   257 *ill-
favoredly* badly

ORLANDO   Just as high as my heart.

JAQUES   You are full of pretty answers. Have you not
been acquainted with goldsmiths' wives, and conned   266
them out of rings?

ORLANDO   Not so; but I answer you right painted cloth,   268
from whence you have studied your questions.

JAQUES   You have a nimble wit; I think 'twas made of   270
Atalanta's heels. Will you sit down with me? and we   271
two will rail against our mistress the world and all our
misery.

ORLANDO   I will chide no breather in the world but my-   274
self, against whom I know most faults.

JAQUES   The worst fault you have is to be in love.

ORLANDO   'Tis a fault I will not change for your best
virtue. I am weary of you.

JAQUES   By my troth, I was seeking for a fool when I
found you.   280

ORLANDO   He is drowned in the brook. Look but in and
you shall see him.

JAQUES   There I shall see mine own figure.

ORLANDO   Which I take to be either a fool or a cipher.   284

JAQUES   I'll tarry no longer with you. Farewell, good
Signor Love.

ORLANDO   I am glad of your departure. Adieu, good
Monsieur Melancholy.   *[Exit Jaques.]*

ROSALIND   I will speak to him like a saucy lackey, and   289
under that habit play the knave with him. Do you hear,   290
forester?

ORLANDO   Very well. What would you?

ROSALIND   I pray you, what is't o'clock?

266–67 *conned . . . rings* memorized them from the verses engraved in rings
268 *right painted cloth* i.e., in the same sort of stock phrases included on
painted wallhangings   271 *Atalanta's heels* (Atalanta was speedy enough to
outrun her suitors)   274 *breather* living creature   284 *cipher* zero   289
saucy lackey smart-mouthed servant   290 *under that habit* (1) in that role,
(2) while wearing that costume; *play the knave* (1) act like a boy, (2) trick

ORLANDO   You should ask me, what time o' day. There's no clock in the forest.

ROSALIND   Then there is no true lover in the forest, else sighing every minute and groaning every hour would
298   detect the lazy foot of Time as well as a clock.

ORLANDO   And why not the swift foot of Time? Had not
300   that been as proper?

ROSALIND   By no means, sir. Time travels in divers paces
302   with divers persons. I'll tell you who Time ambles withal, who Time trots withal, who Time gallops withal, and who he stands still withal.

ORLANDO   I prithee, who doth he trot withal?

306   ROSALIND   Marry, he trots hard with a young maid be-
307   tween the contract of her marriage and the day it is sol-
308   emnized. If the interim be but a sennight, Time's pace is so hard that it seems the length of seven year.

310   ORLANDO   Who ambles Time withal?

ROSALIND   With a priest that lacks Latin and a rich man that hath not the gout; for the one sleeps easily because he cannot study, and the other lives merrily because he feels no pain; the one lacking the burden of lean and
315   wasteful learning, the other knowing no burden of heavy tedious penury. These Time ambles withal.

ORLANDO   Who doth he gallop withal?

ROSALIND   With a thief to the gallows; for though he go
319   as softly as foot can fall, he thinks himself too soon
320   there.

ORLANDO   Who stays it still withal?

ROSALIND   With lawyers in the vacation; for they sleep
323   between term and term, and then they perceive not how time moves.

ORLANDO   Where dwell you, pretty youth?

---

298 *detect* call attention to   302 *withal* with   306 *hard* tortuously   307–8
solemnized celebrated   308 *sennight* week   315 *wasteful* causing one to
waste away   319 *softly* slowly   323 *term* court session

ROSALIND   With this shepherdess, my sister; here in the
skirts of the forest, like fringe upon a petticoat.   327

ORLANDO   Are you native of this place?

ROSALIND   As the cony that you see dwell where she is   329
kindled.   330

ORLANDO   Your accent is something finer than you
could purchase in so removed a dwelling.   332

ROSALIND   I have been told so of many. But indeed an
old religious uncle of mine taught me to speak, who   334
was in his youth an inland man; one that knew   335
courtship too well, for there he fell in love. I have heard   336
him read many lectures against it; and I thank God
I am not a woman, to be touched with so many giddy   338
offenses as he hath generally taxed their whole sex
withal.   340

ORLANDO   Can you remember any of the principal evils
that he laid to the charge of women?

ROSALIND   There were none principal. They were all like
one another as halfpence are, every one fault seeming
monstrous till his fellow fault came to match it.

ORLANDO   I prithee recount some of them.

ROSALIND   No, I will not cast away my physic but on   347
those that are sick. There is a man haunts the forest that
abuses our young plants with carving "Rosalind" on
their barks, hangs odes upon hawthorns, and elegies on   350
brambles; all, forsooth, deifying the name of Rosalind.
If I could meet that fancy-monger, I would give him   352
some good counsel, for he seems to have the quotidian   353
of love upon him.

ORLANDO   I am he that is so love-shaked. I pray you tell
me your remedy.

---

327 *skirts* outskirts, edges 329 *cony* rabbit 330 *kindled* born 332 *purchase* acquire; *removed* remote 334 *religious* in holy orders 335 *inland man* an inhabitant of the town or a courtier 336 *courtship* (1) courtliness, (2) wooing 338 *touched* tainted 347 *physic* medicine; *but* except 352 *fancy-monger* i.e., one who advertises or trades in his so-called love 353 *quotidian* daily fever

ROSALIND   There is none of my uncle's marks upon you.
He taught me how to know a man in love; in which
359   cage of rushes I am sure you are not prisoner.

360   ORLANDO   What were his marks?

361   ROSALIND   A lean cheek, which you have not; a blue eye
362   and sunken, which you have not; an unquestionable
spirit, which you have not; a beard neglected, which
you have not: but I pardon you for that, for simply
365   your having in beard is a younger brother's revenue.
Then your hose should be ungartered, your bonnet un-
banded, your sleeve unbuttoned, your shoe untied, and
everything about you demonstrating a careless desola-
369   tion. But you are no such man: you are rather point-
370   device in your accoutrements, as loving yourself than
seeming the lover of any other.

ORLANDO   Fair youth, I would I could make thee believe
I love.

ROSALIND   Me believe it? You may as soon make her that
you love believe it, which I warrant she is apter to do
than to confess she does; that is one of the points in the
377   which women still give the lie to their consciences. But
in good sooth, are you he that hangs the verses on the
trees wherein Rosalind is so admired?

380   ORLANDO   I swear to thee, youth, by the white hand of
Rosalind, I am that he, that unfortunate he.

ROSALIND   But are you so much in love as your rhymes
speak?

ORLANDO   Neither rhyme nor reason can express how
much.

ROSALIND   Love is merely a madness, and, I tell you, de-
387   serves as well a dark house and a whip as madmen do;

---

359 *cage of rushes* flimsy prison   361 *blue eye* i.e., with dark circles under the
eyes   362 *unquestionable* unwilling to talk   365 *your having . . . revenue* you
have so scant a beard because you are young   369–70 *point-device . . . accoutrements* perfect in your dress   377 *still* always   387 *a dark . . . whip*
(close confinement and whipping were two common treatments for mental
illness)

and the reason why they are not so punished and cured
is that the lunacy is so ordinary that the whippers are in
love too. Yet I profess curing it by counsel.   390

ORLANDO   Did you ever cure any so?

ROSALIND   Yes, one, and in this manner. He was to imagine me his love, his mistress; and I set him every day to
woo me. At which time would I, being but a moonish   394
youth, grieve, be effeminate, changeable, longing and   395
liking, proud, fantastical, apish, shallow, inconstant,   396
full of tears, full of smiles; for every passion something
and for no passion truly anything, as boys and women
are for the most part cattle of this color; would now like
him, now loathe him; then entertain him, then for-   400
swear him; now weep for him, then spit at him; that I
drove my suitor from his mad humor of love to a living   402
humor of madness, which was, to forswear the full
stream of the world and to live in a nook merely
monastic. And thus I cured him; and this way will I
take upon me to wash your liver as clean as a sound   406
sheep's heart, that there shall not be one spot of
love in't.

ORLANDO   I would not be cured, youth.

ROSALIND   I would cure you, if you would but call me   410
Rosalind and come every day to my cote and woo me.   411

ORLANDO   Now, by the faith of my love, I will. Tell me
where it is.

ROSALIND   Go with me to it, and I'll show it you; and by
the way you shall tell me where in the forest you live.
Will you go?

ORLANDO   With all my heart, good youth.

ROSALIND   Nay, you must call me Rosalind. Come, sister, will you go?   *Exeunt.*

---

394 *moonish* fickle   395 *effeminate* like a woman (i.e., ll. 395–98)   396
fantastical irrational; *apish* witlessly imitative   402 *humor* whim   402–3
living humor actual state   406 *liver* (supposed to be the source of the pas-
sions, especially love); *sound* healthy   411 *cote* cottage

✳

✺ **III.3** *Enter [Touchstone the] Clown, Audrey; and*
Jaques [apart].

TOUCHSTONE   Come apace, good Audrey. I will fetch up
   your goats, Audrey. And how, Audrey, am I the man
3   yet? Doth my simple feature content you?
4 AUDREY   Your features, Lord warrant us! What features?
5 TOUCHSTONE   I am here with thee and thy goats, as the
6   most capricious poet, honest Ovid, was among the
   Goths.
8 JAQUES   *[Aside]* O knowledge ill-inhabited, worse than
9   Jove in a thatched house!
10 TOUCHSTONE   When a man's verses cannot be under-
11   stood, nor a man's good wit seconded with the forward
   child, understanding, it strikes a man more dead than a
   great reckoning in a little room. Truly, I would the gods
   had made thee poetical.
   AUDREY   I do not know what poetical is. Is it honest in
   deed and word? Is it a true thing?
   TOUCHSTONE   No, truly; for the truest poetry is the
18   most feigning, and lovers are given to poetry, and what
   they swear in poetry it may be said, as lovers, they do
20   feign.
   AUDREY   Do you wish then that the gods had made me
   poetical?

III.3 The forest   **3** *simple feature* plain appearance   **4** *warrant* protect   **5–7**
goats . . . Goths (Ovid was exiled among the Goths, here pronounced "goats")
6 *capricious* (1) randy, (2) whimsical, (3) goatlike   **8** *ill-inhabited* poorly
lodged   **9** *Jove . . . house* (according to Ovid's *Metamorphoses,* Book VIII,
Jupiter, or Jove, in human form, was once entertained by two peasants, Bau-
cis and Philemon, in their thatched cottage)   **11** *seconded with* acknowl-
edged by   **18** *feigning* (1) imaginative, (2) deceptive

TOUCHSTONE   I do truly; for thou swearest to me thou
   art honest. Now if thou wert a poet, I might have some   24
   hope thou didst feign.

AUDREY   Would you not have me honest?

TOUCHSTONE   No, truly, unless thou wert hard-favored;   27
   for honesty coupled to beauty is to have honey a sauce   28
   to sugar.

JAQUES   *[Aside]* A material fool.   30

AUDREY   Well, I am not fair, and therefore I pray the
   gods make me honest.

TOUCHSTONE   Truly, and to cast away honesty upon a
   foul slut were to put good meat into an unclean dish.   34

AUDREY   I am not a slut, though I thank the gods I am
   foul.   36

TOUCHSTONE   Well, praised be the gods for thy foulness!
   Sluttishness may come hereafter. But be it as it may be,
   I will marry thee; and to that end I have been with Sir
   Oliver Martext, the vicar of the next village, who hath 40
   promised to meet me in this place of the forest and to
   couple us.

JAQUES   *[Aside]* I would fain see this meeting.   43

AUDREY   Well, the gods give us joy!

TOUCHSTONE   Amen. A man may, if he were of a fearful
   heart, stagger in this attempt; for here we have no tem-
   ple but the wood, no assembly but horn beasts. But   47
   what though? Courage! As horns are odious, they are
   necessary. It is said, "Many a man knows no end of his   49
   goods." Right! Many a man has good horns and knows   50
   no end of them. Well, that is the dowry of his wife; 'tis

---

24 *honest* (1) truthful, (2) chaste   27 *hard-favored* ugly   28 *honesty* chastity
30 *material* making good sense   34 *put . . . dish* (a proverb, one of several in
Touchstone's speeches here)   36 *foul* ugly (Audrey interprets the word as a
compliment)   43 *fain* happily   47 *horn beasts* (throughout this passage
Touchstone plays on the old joke that cuckolds – i.e., men whose wives cheat
on them – sprout horns)   49–50 *Many . . . goods* (a proverbial expression
for a man of incalculable wealth)

52 none of his own getting. Horns. Even so, poor men
    alone. No, no; the noblest deer hath them as huge as
54 the rascal. Is the single man therefore blessed? No; as a
    walled town is more worthier than a village, so is the
    forehead of a married man more honorable than the
57 bare brow of a bachelor; and by how much defense is
    better than no skill, by so much is a horn more precious
59 than to want.
        Enter Sir Oliver Martext.
60 Here comes Sir Oliver. Sir Oliver Martext, you are well
61 met. Will you dispatch us here under this tree, or shall
    we go with you to your chapel?
    OLIVER MARTEXT   Is there none here to give the woman?
    TOUCHSTONE   I will not take her on gift of any man.
    OLIVER MARTEXT   Truly, she must be given, or the mar-
        riage is not lawful.
    JAQUES   *[Comes forward.]* Proceed, proceed; I'll give her.
    TOUCHSTONE   Good even, good Master What-ye-call't.
69 How do you, sir? You are very well met. Goddild you
70 for your last company; I am very glad to see you. Even
71 a toy in hand here, sir. Nay, pray be covered.
    JAQUES   Will you be married, motley?
73 TOUCHSTONE   As the ox hath his bow, sir, the horse his
74 curb, and the falcon her bells, so man hath his desires;
75 and as pigeons bill, so wedlock would be nibbling.
    JAQUES   And will you, being a man of your breeding, be
77 married under a bush like a beggar? Get you to church,
    and have a good priest that can tell you what marriage

---

52 *getting* begetting (he does not procure the horns for himself or beget his
own children)   54 *rascal* inferior deer   57 *defense* i.e., the art of defending
oneself, probably from fencing   59 *to want* i.e., to lack horns   61 *dispatch
us* finish off our business   69 *Goddild* God yield (i.e., reward)   70 *last* recent   71 *toy* unimportant matter; *pray be covered* keep your hat on   73 *bow*
collar of the yoke   74 *curb* bit; *bells* (attached to a falcon's legs so that it can
be more easily identified and reclaimed after a hunt)   75 *bill* rub bills together   77 *married . . . bush* (Oliver is a "hedge-priest" – i.e., uneducated,
unable to expound the obligations of marriage)

is. This fellow will but join you together as they join   79
wainscot; then one of you will prove a shrunk panel,   80
and like green timber warp, warp.   81

TOUCHSTONE   *[Aside]* I am not in the mind but I were   82
better to be married of him than of another; for he is
not like to marry me well; and not being well married,
it will be a good excuse for me hereafter to leave my
wife.

JAQUES   Go thou with me and let me counsel thee.

TOUCHSTONE   Come, sweet Audrey. We must be married, or we must live in bawdry. Fare well, good Master   89
Oliver: not   90

        O sweet Oliver,   91
        O brave Oliver,
        Leave me not behind thee;
but
        Wind away,
        Be gone, I say;
        I will not to wedding with thee.
              Exeunt [Jaques, Touchstone, and Audrey].

OLIVER MARTEXT   'Tis no matter. Ne'er a fantastical   98
knave of them all shall flout me out of my calling.
                         [Exit.]

              *

∾ **III.4** *Enter Rosalind [dressed as Ganymede] and Celia
[dressed as Aliena].*

ROSALIND   Never talk to me; I will weep.

CELIA   Do, I prithee; but yet have the grace to consider
that tears do not become a man.

ROSALIND   But have I not cause to weep?

79–80 *as . . . wainscot* i.e., as they set paneling together, without joining it
securely **81** *warp* (and therefore move out of alignment and fit) **82** *I . . .
were* I am not sure that I won't be **89** *bawdry* immorality **91–97** *O sweet
Oliver . . .* (fragments from a popular ballad) **98** *fantastical* wacky
  III.4 The forest

CELIA As good cause as one would desire; therefore weep.

7 ROSALIND His very hair is of the dissembling color.

CELIA Something browner than Judas's. Marry, his kisses
9 are Judas's own children.

10 ROSALIND I' faith, his hair is of a good color.

CELIA An excellent color. Your chestnut was ever the only color.

ROSALIND And his kissing is as full of sanctity as the touch of holy bread.

15 CELIA He hath bought a pair of cast lips of Diana. A nun
16 of winter's sisterhood kisses not more religiously; the very ice of chastity is in them.

ROSALIND But why did he swear he would come this morning, and comes not?

20 CELIA Nay, certainly there is no truth in him.

ROSALIND Do you think so?

CELIA Yes; I think he is not a pickpurse nor a horse
23 stealer, but for his verity in love, I do think him as concave as a covered goblet or a worm-eaten nut.

ROSALIND Not true in love?

CELIA Yes, when he is in, but I think he is not in.

ROSALIND You have heard him swear downright he was.

CELIA "Was" is not "is." Besides, the oath of a lover is no
29 stronger than the word of a tapster; they are both the
30 confirmer of false reckonings. He attends here in the forest on the duke your father.

ROSALIND I met the duke yesterday and had much question with him. He asked me of what parentage I was. I told him, of as good as he; so he laughed and let me go.

---

7 *dissembling color* i.e., reddish, the traditional color of Judas's hair 9 *Judas's own children* i.e., offspring of a betrayer 15 *cast* (1) discarded, (2) sculpted (perhaps with a play on "chaste" – Diana was the goddess of chastity) 16 *of winter's sisterhood* i.e., sworn to coldness 23–24 *concave* hollow 29 *tapster* bartender 30 *reckonings* accounts (see Matthew 26:48–49) 30–31 *attends . . . on* serves

But what talk we of fathers when there is such a man as
Orlando?

CELIA   O, that's a brave man; he writes brave verses,   37
speaks brave words, swears brave oaths, and breaks
them bravely, quite traverse, athwart the heart of his   39
lover, as a puny tilter, that spurs his horse but on one   40
side, breaks his staff like a noble goose. But all's brave   41
that youth mounts and folly guides. Who comes here?
    Enter Corin.

CORIN
Mistress and master, you have oft inquired
After the shepherd that complained of love,
Who you saw sitting by me on the turf,
Praising the proud disdainful shepherdess
That was his mistress.

CELIA   Well, and what of him?

CORIN
If you will see a pageant truly played   48
Between the pale complexion of true love
And the red glow of scorn and proud disdain,   50
Go hence a little, and I shall conduct you,
If you will mark it.   52

ROSALIND   O, come, let us remove:
The sight of lovers feedeth those in love.
Bring us to this sight, and you shall say
I'll prove a busy actor in their play.   *Exeunt.*
                        *

∾ **III.5** *Enter Silvius and Phebe.*

SILVIUS
Sweet Phebe, do not scorn me; do not, Phebe!

---

37 *brave* excellent   39 *traverse* (a term in tilting, for hitting an opponent
sideways, awkwardly, instead of head-on)   40 *but* only   41 *noble goose*
grand fool   48 *pageant* performance   52 *mark* observe; *remove* go
    III.5 The forest

Say that you love me not, but say not so
In bitterness. The common executioner,
Whose heart th' accustomed sight of death makes hard,
5   Falls not the ax upon the humbled neck
But first begs pardon. Will you sterner be
7   Than he that dies and lives by bloody drops?
          *Enter [apart] Rosalind [dressed as Ganymede], Celia
          [dressed as Aliena], and Corin.*

PHEBE
I would not be thy executioner.
I fly thee, for I would not injure thee.
10   Thou tell'st me there is murder in mine eye:
'Tis pretty, sure, and very probable
That eyes, that are the frail'st and softest things,
13   Who shut their coward gates on atomies,
Should be called tyrants, butchers, murderers.
Now I do frown on thee with all my heart,
And if mine eyes can wound, now let them kill thee.
17   Now counterfeit to swoon; why, now fall down;
Or if thou canst not, O, for shame, for shame,
Lie not, to say mine eyes are murderers.
20   Now show the wound mine eye hath made in thee;
Scratch thee but with a pin, and there remains
Some scar of it; lean upon a rush,
23   The cicatrice and capable impressure
Thy palm some moment keeps; but now mine eyes,
Which I have darted at thee, hurt thee not,
Nor I am sure there is no force in eyes
That can do hurt.

SILVIUS   O dear Phebe,
If ever, as that ever may be near,
29   You meet in some fresh cheek the power of fancy,
30   Then shall you know the wounds invisible

---

5 *Falls* lets fall   **7** *dies* kills; *lives* makes his living   **13** *atomies* motes   **17**
counterfeit to pretend to   **23** *cicatrice* mark (literally, scar); *capable impressure*
visible impression   **29** *fancy* love

That love's keen arrows make.

PHEBE   But till that time
Come not thou near me; and when that time comes,
Afflict me with thy mocks, pity me not,
As till that time I shall not pity thee.

ROSALIND
And why, I pray you? Who might be your mother,
That you insult, exult, and all at once,
Over the wretched? What though you have no beauty
(As, by my faith, I see no more in you
Than without candle may go dark to bed)   39
Must you be therefore proud and pitiless?   40
Why, what means this? Why do you look on me?
I see no more in you than in the ordinary   42
Of nature's salework. 'Od's my little life,   43
I think she means to tangle my eyes too!   44
No, faith, proud mistress, hope not after it;
'Tis not your inky brows, your black silk hair,
Your bugle eyeballs, nor your cheek of cream   47
That can entame my spirits to your worship.
You foolish shepherd, wherefore do you follow her,
Like foggy south, puffing with wind and rain?   50
You are a thousand times a properer man   51
Than she a woman. 'Tis such fools as you
That makes the world full of ill-favored children.
'Tis not her glass, but you, that flatters her,   54
And out of you she sees herself more proper   55
Than any of her lineaments can show her.
But mistress, know yourself. Down on your knees,
And thank heaven, fasting, for a good man's love;
For I must tell you friendly in your ear,
Sell when you can, you are not for all markets.   60

---

39 *Than . . . bed* (than could light your way to bed in the dark) 42 *ordinary* common run 43 *salework* ready-made products, not distinctive; *'Od's . . . life* God save me 44 *tangle* trap 47 *bugle* like black glass 50 *south* south wind 51 *properer* more handsome 54 *glass* mirror 55 *out of you* reflected through you

61 Cry the man mercy, love him, take his offer;
62 Foul is most foul, being foul to be a scoffer;
    So take her to thee, shepherd. Fare you well.

PHEBE
    Sweet youth, I pray you chide a year together;
    I had rather hear you chide than this man woo.

ROSALIND *[Aside]* He's fallen in love with your foulness,
    and she'll fall in love with my anger. If it be so, as
68 fast as she answers thee with frowning looks, I'll sauce
    her with bitter words. *[To Phebe]* Why look you so
70 upon me?

PHEBE
    For no ill will I bear you.

ROSALIND
    I pray you do not fall in love with me,
    For I am falser than vows made in wine.
    Besides, I like you not. If you will know my house,
75 'Tis at the tuft of olives, here hard by.
    Will you go, sister? Shepherd, ply her hard.
    Come, sister. Shepherdess, look on him better
    And be not proud. Though all the world could see,
    None could be so abused in sight as he.
80 Come, to our flock.   *Exit [with Celia and Corin].*

PHEBE
81 Dead shepherd, now I find thy saw of might,
82 "Who ever loved that loved not at first sight?"

SILVIUS
    Sweet Phebe.

PHEBE   Ha! what say'st thou, Silvius?

SILVIUS
    Sweet Phebe, pity me.

---

61 *Cry . . . mercy* beg the man's pardon **62** *Foul . . . scoffer* ugliness is most
repulsive when it is disdainful **68** *sauce* rebuke **75** *olives* olive trees; *hard*
near **81** *Dead shepherd* Christopher Marlowe (here referred to as a pastoral
poet), who was killed in 1593; *saw* saying; *might* power **82** *"Who . . . sight"*
(Marlowe's *Hero and Leander* [published 1598], I, 176)

PHEBE

Why, I am sorry for thee, gentle Silvius.

SILVIUS

Wherever sorrow is, relief would be.
If you do sorrow at my grief in love,
By giving love your sorrow and my grief
Were both extermined.   89

PHEBE

Thou hast my love. Is not that neighborly?   90

SILVIUS

I would have you.

PHEBE   Why, that were covetousness.
Silvius, the time was that I hated thee;
And yet it is not that I bear thee love,   93
But since that thou canst talk of love so well,
Thy company, which erst was irksome to me,   95
I will endure; and I'll employ thee too;
But do not look for further recompense
Than thine own gladness that thou art employed.

SILVIUS

So holy and so perfect is my love,
And I in such a poverty of grace,   100
That I shall think it a most plenteous crop
To glean the broken ears after the man   102
That the main harvest reaps. Loose now and then   103
A scattered smile, and that I'll live upon.

PHEBE

Know'st thou the youth that spoke to me erewhile?

SILVIUS

Not very well, but I have met him oft,
And he hath bought the cottage and the bounds
That the old Carlot once was master of.

---

89 *extermined* eliminated   90 *neighborly* (possibly a reference to the commandment "Thou shalt love thy neighbor as thyself," Matthew 19:19)   93 *yet it is not* the time has not come   95 *erst* once   100 *such . . . grace* so lacking in your favor   102 *broken ears* i.e., of corn   103 *Loose* release

PHEBE

Think not I love him, though I ask for him;

110   'Tis but a peevish boy; yet he talks well.

But what care I for words? Yet words do well

When he that speaks them pleases those that hear.

It is a pretty youth; not very pretty;

But sure he's proud; and yet his pride becomes him.

He'll make a proper man. The best thing in him

Is his complexion; and faster than his tongue

Did make offense, his eye did heal it up.

He is not very tall; yet for his years he's tall.

His leg is but so-so; and yet 'tis well.

120   There was a pretty redness in his lip,

A little riper and more lusty red

Than that mixed in his cheek; 'twas just the difference

123   Betwixt the constant red and mingled damask.

There be some women, Silvius, had they marked him

125   In parcels as I did, would have gone near

To fall in love with him; but, for my part,

I love him not nor hate him not; and yet

I have more cause to hate him than to love him;

For what had he to do to chide at me?

130   He said mine eyes were black and my hair black;

131   And, now I am remembered, scorned at me.

I marvel why I answered not again.

133   But that's all one: omittance is no quittance.

I'll write to him a very taunting letter,

And thou shalt bear it. Wilt thou, Silvius?

SILVIUS

136   Phebe, with all my heart.

PHEBE   I'll write it straight;

137   The matter's in my head and in my heart;

---

123 *mingled damask* pink and white (the colors of damask roses) **125** *In parcels* part by part **131** *remembered* reminded **133** *omittance is no quittance* i.e., failure to assert one's rights is not renunciation of them (proverbial) **136** *straight* straightaway, immediately **137** *the matter* what I plan to say

I will be bitter with him and passing short.   138
Go with me, Silvius.   *Exeunt.*

                              *

∾ **IV.1** *Enter Rosalind [dressed as Ganymede], Celia
[dressed as Aliena], and Jaques.*

JAQUES   I prithee, pretty youth, let me be better ac-
quainted with thee.
ROSALIND   They say you are a melancholy fellow.
JAQUES   I am so; I do love it better than laughing.
ROSALIND   Those that are in extremity of either are   5
abominable fellows, and betray themselves to every
modern censure worse than drunkards.   7
JAQUES   Why, 'tis good to be sad and say nothing.
ROSALIND   Why then, 'tis good to be a post.
JAQUES   I have neither the scholar's melancholy, which is   10
emulation; nor the musician's, which is fantastical; nor   11
the courtier's, which is proud; nor the soldier's, which is
ambitious; nor the lawyer's, which is politic; nor the   13
lady's, which is nice; nor the lover's, which is all these: 14
but it is a melancholy of mine own, compounded of
many simples, extracted from many objects, and in-   16
deed the sundry contemplation of my travels, which,   17
by often rumination, wraps me in a most humorous   18
sadness.
ROSALIND   A traveler! By my faith, you have great reason   20
to be sad. I fear you have sold your own lands to see
other men's. Then to have seen much and to have nothing is to have rich eyes and poor hands.
JAQUES   Yes, I have gained my experience.
          Enter Orlando.

---

138 *passing short* extremely curt
   IV.1 The forest   5 *are in extremity* go to extremes   7 *modern censure*
common criticism   11 *emulation* envy; *fantastical* absurdly elaborate   13
politic sneaky, clever   14 *nice* overrefined   16 *simples* ingredients   17
sundry diverse   18 *humorous* moody

ROSALIND   And your experience makes you sad. I had
rather have a fool to make me merry than experience to
27 make me sad: and to travel for it too.

ORLANDO   Good day and happiness, dear Rosalind.

29 JAQUES   Nay then, God b' wi' you, an you talk in blank
30 verse.

31 ROSALIND   Farewell, Monsieur Traveler. Look you lisp
32 and wear strange suits, disable all the benefits of your
33 own country, be out of love with your nativity, and al-
34 most chide God for making you that countenance you
35 are; or I will scarce think you have swam in a gondola.

                                        [Exit Jaques.]

Why, how now, Orlando, where have you been all this
while? You a lover? An you serve me such another trick,
never come in my sight more.

ORLANDO   My fair Rosalind, I come within an hour of
40 my promise.

ROSALIND   Break an hour's promise in love? He that will
divide a minute into a thousand parts and break but a
part of the thousand part of a minute in the affairs of
44 love, it may be said of him that Cupid hath clapped
him o' th' shoulder, but I'll warrant him heart-whole.

ORLANDO   Pardon me, dear Rosalind.

ROSALIND   Nay, an you be so tardy, come no more in my
48 sight. I had as lief be wooed of a snail.

ORLANDO   Of a snail?

50 ROSALIND   Ay, of a snail; for though he comes slowly, he
51 carries his house on his head; a better jointure, I think,

---

27 *travel* (with a pun on "travail," or labor)   29 *an* if   29–30 *blank verse* un-
rhymed verse, usually in iambic pentameter (most of the poetry in this play
is in blank verse)   31 *Look you* be sure you; *lisp* speak with an affected accent
32 *disable* disparage   33 *nativity* birthplace   34–35 *making . . . are* giving
you the appearance you have   35 *swam in a gondola* ridden in a gondola or
small boat (i.e., have been to Venice)   44–45 *Cupid . . . heart-whole* i.e.,
Cupid has arrested or wounded him, but I'll guarantee that his heart is still
in one piece   48 *of* by   51 *jointure* marriage settlement

than you make a woman. Besides, he brings his destiny
with him.

ORLANDO   What's that?

ROSALIND   Why, horns; which such as you are fain to be   55
beholding to your wives for; but he comes armed in his
fortune and prevents the slander of his wife.   57

ORLANDO   Virtue is no horn-maker, and my Rosalind is
virtuous.

ROSALIND   And I am your Rosalind.   60

CELIA   It pleases him to call you so; but he hath a Rosalind of a better leer than you.   62

ROSALIND   Come, woo me, woo me; for now I am in a
holiday humor and like enough to consent. What
would you say to me now, and I were your very very
Rosalind?

ORLANDO   I would kiss before I spoke.

ROSALIND   Nay, you were better speak first, and when
you were graveled for lack of matter, you might take oc-   69
casion to kiss. Very good orators, when they are out,   70
they will spit; and for lovers, lacking – God warn us! –   71
matter, the cleanliest shift is to kiss.   72

ORLANDO   How if the kiss be denied?

ROSALIND   Then she puts you to entreaty, and there be-   74
gins new matter.

ORLANDO   Who could be out, being before his beloved   76
mistress?

ROSALIND   Marry, that should you, if I were your mis-   78
tress, or I should think my honesty ranker than my wit.   79

ORLANDO   What, of my suit?   80

---

55 *fain* obliged   57 *prevents* forestalls   62 *leer* appearance   69 *graveled*
stuck   70 *out* out of things to say   71 *warn* save   72 *matter* (1) something
to say, (2) bodies; *cleanliest shift* cleverest strategy   74 *puts . . . entreaty* makes
you beg   76 *out* (1) out of things to say, (2) shut out sexually   78 *that . . .
you* you would be   79 *honesty* chastity; *ranker* less pure   80 *suit* plea (but
Rosalind in reply puns on the word)

ROSALIND   Not out of your apparel, and yet out of your
suit. Am not I your Rosalind?

ORLANDO   I take some joy to say you are, because I
would be talking of her.

ROSALIND   Well, in her person, I say I will not have you.

ORLANDO   Then, in mine own person, I die.

87   ROSALIND   No, faith, die by attorney. The poor world is
88   almost six thousand years old, and in all this time there
89   was not any man died in his own person, videlicet, in a
90   love cause. Troilus had his brains dashed out with a
Grecian club; yet he did what he could to die before,
92   and he is one of the patterns of love. Leander, he would
have lived many a fair year though Hero had turned
nun, if it had not been for a hot midsummer night; for,
good youth, he went but forth to wash him in the
Hellespont, and being taken with the cramp, was
97   drowned; and the foolish chroniclers of that age found
it was "Hero of Sestos." But these are all lies. Men have
died from time to time, and worms have eaten them,
100   but not for love.

101   ORLANDO   I would not have my right Rosalind of this
mind, for I protest her frown might kill me.

ROSALIND   By this hand, it will not kill a fly. But come,
104   now I will be your Rosalind in a more coming-on disposition; and ask me what you will, I will grant it.

ORLANDO   Then love me, Rosalind.

ROSALIND   Yes, faith, will I, Fridays and Saturdays and
all.

---

87 *by attorney* by proxy   88 *six thousand* (traditionally, the creation of the
world was dated at approximately 4000 B.C.)   89 *videlicet* namely   90
Troilus the faithful lover of the faithless Cressida, whose story is told by both
Chaucer and Shakespeare (in some versions of the story, although not in
Shakespeare's, the Greek soldier Achilles kills Troilus)   92 *Leander* the faithful lover in classical myth and in Marlowe's *Hero and Leander,* who swam the
Hellespont each night to visit Hero, his beloved, and drowned   97–98
chroniclers . . . Sestos i.e., storytellers said he died for love of Hero from Sestos
101 *right* real   104 *coming-on* yielding

ORLANDO   And wilt thou have me?

ROSALIND   Ay, and twenty such.   *110*

ORLANDO   What sayest thou?

ROSALIND   Are you not good?

ORLANDO   I hope so.

ROSALIND   Why then, can one desire too much of a good thing? Come, sister, you shall be the priest and marry us. Give me your hand, Orlando. What do you say, sister?

ORLANDO   Pray thee marry us.

CELIA   I cannot say the words.

ROSALIND   You must begin, "Will you, Orlando" –

CELIA   Go to. Will you, Orlando, have to wife this Rosa-   *120* lind?

ORLANDO   I will.

ROSALIND   Ay, but when?

ORLANDO   Why now, as fast as she can marry us.

ROSALIND   Then you must say, "I take thee, Rosalind, for wife."

ORLANDO   I take thee, Rosalind, for wife.

ROSALIND   I might ask you for your commission; but I   *128* do take thee, Orlando, for my husband. There's a girl goes before the priest, and certainly a woman's thought   *130* runs before her actions.

ORLANDO   So do all thoughts; they are wingèd.

ROSALIND   Now tell me how long you would have her after you have possessed her.

ORLANDO   For ever and a day.

ROSALIND   Say "a day," without the "ever." No, no, Orlando; men are April when they woo, December when they wed. Maids are May when they are maids, but the sky changes when they are wives. I will be more jealous of thee than a Barbary cock pigeon over his hen, more   *140*

---

120 *Go to* (an expression of impatience, similar to "come on")   128 *commission* authority   130 *goes before* who anticipates   140 *Barbary cock pigeon* (this exotic bird, which originally came from the north of Africa, was traditionally associated with jealousy)

141   clamorous than a parrot against rain, more newfangled
than an ape, more giddy in my desires than a monkey. I
143   will weep for nothing, like Diana in the fountain, and I
will do that when you are disposed to be merry; I will
laugh like a hyena, and that when thou art inclined to
sleep.

ORLANDO   But will my Rosalind do so?

ROSALIND   By my life, she will do as I do.

ORLANDO   O, but she is wise.

150 ROSALIND   Or else she could not have the wit to do this;
151   the wiser, the waywarder. Make the doors upon a
woman's wit, and it will out at the casement; shut that,
and 'twill out at the keyhole; stop that, 'twill fly with
the smoke out at the chimney.

ORLANDO   A man that had a wife with such a wit, he
156   might say, "Wit, whither wilt?"

157 ROSALIND   Nay, you might keep that check for it till you
met your wife's wit going to your neighbor's bed.

ORLANDO   And what wit could wit have to excuse that?

160 ROSALIND   Marry, to say she came to seek you there. You
shall never take her without her answer unless you take
her without her tongue. O, that woman that cannot
163   make her fault her husband's occasion, let her never
164   nurse her child herself, for she will breed it like a fool.

ORLANDO   For these two hours, Rosalind, I will leave
thee.

ROSALIND   Alas, dear love, I cannot lack thee two hours!

ORLANDO   I must attend the duke at dinner. By two
o'clock I will be with thee again.

---

141 *against* in anticipation of; *newfangled* fashion-conscious   143 *Diana in
the fountain* (figures of Diana were often placed at the center of ornamental
fountains)   151 *Make* fasten   156 *whither wilt* where will you go (See
I.2.53–54. We see here the conventional association of women's verbal and
sexual wandering.)   157 *check* retort   163 *make . . . occasion* find a way to
blame her husband for anything she does wrong; *occasion* responsibility
164 *breed* raise

ROSALIND   Ay, go your ways, go your ways; I knew what   *170*
you would prove. My friends told me as much, and I
thought no less. That flattering tongue of yours won
me. 'Tis but one cast away, and so, come death! Two   *173*
o'clock is your hour?

ORLANDO   Ay, sweet Rosalind.

ROSALIND   By my troth, and in good earnest, and so God
mend me, and by all pretty oaths that are not dangerous, if you break one jot of your promise or come one
minute behind your hour, I will think you the most pa-   *179*
thetical break-promise, and the most hollow lover, and   *180*
the most unworthy of her you call Rosalind, that may
be chosen out of the gross band of the unfaithful.   *182*
Therefore beware my censure and keep your promise.

ORLANDO   With no less religion than if thou wert indeed   *184*
my Rosalind. So adieu.

ROSALIND   Well, Time is the old justice that examines all
such offenders, and let Time try. Adieu. *Exit [Orlando].*   *187*

CELIA   You have simply misused our sex in your love   *188*
prate. We must have your doublet and hose plucked
over your head, and show the world what the bird hath   *190*
done to her own nest.

ROSALIND   O coz, coz, coz, my pretty little coz, that thou
didst know how many fathom deep I am in love! But it
cannot be sounded. My affection hath an unknown   *194*
bottom, like the Bay of Portugal.   *195*

CELIA   Or rather, bottomless, that as fast as you pour affection in, it runs out.

ROSALIND   No, that same wicked bastard of Venus that   *198*
was begot of thought, conceived of spleen, and born of   *199*

---

173 *'Tis . . . away* it is just one more seduced and abandoned woman
179–80 *pathetical* pitiful   182 *gross band* whole group   184 *With . . . reli-*
gion no less religiously   187 *try* test, judge ("time tries all things" is proverbial)   188 *misused* slandered   194 *sounded* plumbed to its depths   195 *Bay*
of Portugal (considered to be very deep)   198 *bastard of Venus* Cupid, who
was Venus's son by her lover, Mercury, rather than her husband, Vulcan
199 *thought* imagination; *spleen* impulse

200 madness, that blind rascally boy that abuses every one's
eyes because his own are out, let him be judge how
deep I am in love. I'll tell thee, Aliena, I cannot be out
203 of the sight of Orlando. I'll go find a shadow, and sigh
till he come.

CELIA And I'll sleep.   *Exeunt.*

*

❧ **IV.2** *Enter Jaques; and Lords [dressed as] Foresters.*

JAQUES Which is he that killed the deer?

[FIRST] LORD Sir, it was I.

JAQUES Let's present him to the duke like a Roman con-
queror; and it would do well to set the deer's horns
upon his head for a branch of victory. Have you no
song, forester, for this purpose?

[SECOND] LORD Yes, sir.

JAQUES Sing it. 'Tis no matter how it be in tune, so it
make noise enough.

      Music.

[SECOND LORD] *[Sings.]*

10   What shall he have that killed the deer?
      His leather skin and horns to wear:
12   Then sing him home; the rest shall bear this burden.
      Take thou no scorn to wear the horn,
      It was a crest ere thou wast born,
          Thy father's father wore it,
          And thy father bore it.
      The horn, the horn, the lusty horn,
      Is not a thing to laugh to scorn.   *Exeunt.*

*

---

200 *abuses* deceives **203** *shadow* some shade
      IV.2 The forest **10–18** *What . . . scorn* (the song builds on the many
cuckold/horn jokes in the play) **12** *burden* (1) load, (2) refrain of a song

❧ **IV.3** *Enter Rosalind [dressed as Ganymede] and Celia [dressed as Aliena].*

ROSALIND   How say you now, is it not past two o'clock?
And here much Orlando!   2
CELIA   I warrant you, with pure love and troubled brain,
he hath ta'en his bow and arrows and is gone forth to
sleep.
        Enter Silvius.
Look who comes here.
SILVIUS
My errand is to you, fair youth.
My gentle Phebe did bid me give you this.
        [Gives a letter.]
I know not the contents, but, as I guess
By the stern brow and waspish action   10
Which she did use as she was writing of it,
It bears an angry tenor. Pardon me;
I am but as a guiltless messenger.
ROSALIND
Patience herself would startle at this letter
And play the swaggerer. Bear this, bear all!
She says I am not fair, that I lack manners;
She calls me proud, and that she could not love me,
Were man as rare as phoenix. 'Od's my will!   18
Her love is not the hare that I do hunt.
Why writes she so to me? Well, shepherd, well,   20
This is a letter of your own device.   21
SILVIUS
No, I protest, I know not the contents.
Phebe did write it.
ROSALIND   Come, come, you are a fool,

IV.3 The forest   2 *much Orlando* i.e., no Orlando   18 *Were . . . as* if men
were as; *phoenix* (there was supposed to be only one phoenix in the world at
a time); *'Od's* God save (an oath expressing exasperation)   21 *device* devising

24   And turned into the extremity of love.
       I saw her hand. She has a leathern hand,
26   A freestone-colored hand. I verily did think
       That her old gloves were on, but 'twas her hands.
       She has a housewife's hand; but that's no matter:
       I say she never did invent this letter;
30   This is a man's invention and his hand.
SILVIUS
       Sure it is hers.
ROSALIND
       Why, 'tis a boisterous and a cruel style,
       A style for challengers. Why, she defies me
34   Like Turk to Christian. Women's gentle brain
35   Could not drop forth such giant-rude invention,
36   Such Ethiop words, blacker in their effect
       Than in their countenance. Will you hear the letter?
SILVIUS
       So please you, for I never heard it yet;
       Yet heard too much of Phebe's cruelty.
ROSALIND
40   She Phebes me. Mark how the tyrant writes.
           Read[s].
               "Art thou god, to shepherd turned,
               That a maiden's heart hath burned?"
       Can a woman rail thus?
SILVIUS   Call you this railing?
ROSALIND   *Read[s].*

---

24 *turned into* brought to; *extremity* great intensity   26 *freestone* soft sand-
stone or limestone, yellowish brown   34 *Turk to Christian* (Turks were
viewed as a particular threat to Christian countries in Western Europe; they
were also frequently represented as the demonic opposite of Christianity)
35 *giant-rude* very crude or violent   36 *Ethiop* (1) black from ink, (2)
strange or evil (investing color with moral, and gradually racial, significance,
Elizabethans associated blackness with evil and whiteness with virtue)   40
Phebes me i.e., addresses me with her characteristic cruelty

"Why, thy godhead laid apart,   44
Warr'st thou with a woman's heart?"
Did you ever hear such railing?
"Whiles the eye of man did woo me,
That could do no vengeance to me."   48
Meaning me a beast.
"If the scorn of your bright eyne   50
Have power to raise such love in mine,
Alack, in me what strange effect
Would they work in mild aspect!   53
Whiles you chid me, I did love;
How then might your prayers move!
He that brings this love to thee
Little knows this love in me;
And by him seal up thy mind,   58
Whether that thy youth and kind   59
Will the faithful offer take   60
Of me and all that I can make,
Or else by him my love deny,
And then I'll study how to die."

SILVIUS
Call you this chiding?
CELIA   Alas, poor shepherd!
ROSALIND   Do you pity him? No, he deserves no pity.
Wilt thou love such a woman? What, to make thee an   66
instrument, and play false strains upon thee? Not to be
endured! Well, go your way to her, for I see love hath
made thee a tame snake, and say this to her: that if she   69
love me, I charge her to love thee; if she will not, I will 70
never have her unless thou entreat for her. If you be a

---

44 *thy . . . apart* i.e., as a god who has assumed human form   48 *vengeance*
harm   50 *eyne* eyes (archaic form)   53 *in mild aspect* i.e., if they looked on
me pleasantly   58 *seal . . . mind* enclose your thoughts in a letter   59 *youth
and kind* youthful nature   66–67 *make . . . upon thee* use you (with a pun on
instrument) and deceive you at the same time   69 *snake* i.e., the lowest kind
of creature (perhaps with a reference to impotence)

true lover, hence, and not a word; for here comes more
company.   *Exit Silvius.*
    Enter Oliver.

OLIVER
Good morrow, fair ones. Pray you, if you know,
75 Where in the purlieus of this forest stands
A sheepcote, fenced about with olive trees?

CELIA
77 West of this place, down in the neighbor bottom.
78 The rank of osiers by the murmuring stream
Left on your right hand brings you to the place.
80 But at this hour the house doth keep itself;
There's none within.

OLIVER
If that an eye may profit by a tongue,
Then should I know you by description,
Such garments and such years: "The boy is fair,
85 Of female favor, and bestows himself
86 Like a ripe sister; the woman low,
And browner than her brother." Are not you
The owner of the house I did inquire for?

CELIA
It is no boast, being asked, to say we are.

OLIVER
90 Orlando doth commend him to you both,
And to that youth he calls his Rosalind
92 He sends this bloody napkin. Are you he?

ROSALIND
I am. What must we understand by this?

OLIVER
Some of my shame, if you will know of me
What man I am, and how and why and where
This handkerchief was stained.

---

75 *in the purlieus* within the borders   77 *neighbor bottom* nearby valley   78
rank of osiers row of willows   85 *favor* features; *bestows* conducts   86 *ripe*
mature; *low* short   92 *napkin* handkerchief

CELIA   I pray you tell it.
OLIVER
    When last the young Orlando parted from you,
    He left a promise to return again
    Within an hour; and pacing through the forest,
    Chewing the food of sweet and bitter fancy,   100
    Lo, what befell! He threw his eye aside,
    And mark what object did present itself:
    Under an old oak, whose boughs were mossed with age
    And high top bald with dry antiquity,
    A wretched ragged man, o'ergrown with hair,
    Lay sleeping on his back; about his neck
    A green and gilded snake had wreathed itself,
    Who with her head, nimble in threats, approached
    The opening of his mouth; but suddenly,
    Seeing Orlando, it unlinked itself   110
    And with indented glides did slip away   111
    Into a bush, under which bush's shade
    A lioness, with udders all drawn dry,   113
    Lay couching, head on ground, with catlike watch   114
    When that the sleeping man should stir; for 'tis
    The royal disposition of that beast
    To prey on nothing that doth seem as dead.
    This seen, Orlando did approach the man
    And found it was his brother, his elder brother.
CELIA
    O, I have heard him speak of that same brother,   120
    And he did render him the most unnatural   121
    That lived amongst men.
OLIVER   And well he might so do,
    For well I know he was unnatural.
ROSALIND
    But, to Orlando: did he leave him there,

----

110 *unlinked* uncoiled   111 *indented* sinuous   113 *udders . . . dry* i.e., having nursed her cubs, the lion would be very hungry   114 *couching* crouched
121 *render* describe

125   Food to the sucked and hungry lioness?

OLIVER
126   Twice did he turn his back and purposed so;
127   But kindness, nobler ever than revenge,
128   And nature, stronger than his just occasion,
        Made him give battle to the lioness,
130   Who quickly fell before him; in which hurtling
        From miserable slumber I awaked.

CELIA
        Are you his brother?

ROSALIND   Was't you he rescued?

CELIA
        Was't you that did so oft contrive to kill him?

OLIVER
        'Twas I. But 'tis not I. I do not shame
        To tell you what I was, since my conversion
        So sweetly tastes, being the thing I am.

ROSALIND
137   But, for the bloody napkin?

OLIVER   By and by.
        When from the first to last, betwixt us two,
139   Tears our recountments had most kindly bathed,
140   As how I came into that desert place:
        In brief, he led me to the gentle duke,
142   Who gave me fresh array and entertainment,
        Committing me unto my brother's love,
        Who led me instantly unto his cave,
        There stripped himself, and here upon his arm
        The lioness had torn some flesh away,
        Which all this while had bled; and now he fainted,
        And cried, in fainting, upon Rosalind.

---

125 *sucked* sucked dry   126 *purposed so* intended to   127 *kindness* (1) familial affection, (2) natural inclination   128 *just occasion* justifiable excuse (for leaving Oliver to the lion)   130 *hurtling* tumult   137 *for* what about; *By and by* in a minute   139 *recountments* accounts (of events since we separated)   142 *array* clothes; *entertainment* food and drink

Brief, I recovered him, bound up his wound;   149
And after some small space, being strong at heart,   150
He sent me hither, stranger as I am,
To tell this story, that you might excuse
His broken promise, and to give this napkin,
Dyed in his blood, unto the shepherd youth
That he in sport doth call his Rosalind.
    [Rosalind faints.]

CELIA
Why, how now, Ganymede, sweet Ganymede!

OLIVER
Many will swoon when they do look on blood.

CELIA
There is more in it. Cousin Ganymede!

OLIVER
Look, he recovers.

ROSALIND
I would I were at home.   160

CELIA   We'll lead you thither.
I pray you, will you take him by the arm?

OLIVER   Be of good cheer, youth. You a man! You lack a
man's heart.

ROSALIND   I do so, I confess it. Ah, sirrah, a body would
think this was well counterfeited. I pray you tell your   165
brother how well I counterfeited. Heigh-ho!

OLIVER   This was not counterfeit. There is too great testimony in your complexion that it was a passion of   168
earnest.

ROSALIND   Counterfeit, I assure you.   170

OLIVER   Well then, take a good heart and counterfeit to
be a man.

ROSALIND   So I do; but, i' faith, I should have been a
woman by right.

---

149 *Brief* in brief; *recovered* revived 165 *counterfeited* acted, pretended
168–69 *passion of earnest* display of genuine emotion

CELIA   Come, you look paler and paler. Pray you draw
homewards. Good sir, go with us.

OLIVER
That will I, for I must bear answer back
How you excuse my brother, Rosalind.

ROSALIND   I shall devise something. But I pray you com-
180   mend my counterfeiting to him. Will you go?   *Exeunt.*

*

∾ **V.1** *Enter [Touchstone the] Clown and Audrey.*

TOUCHSTONE   We shall find a time, Audrey. Patience,
gentle Audrey.

AUDREY   Faith, the priest was good enough, for all the
old gentleman's saying.

TOUCHSTONE   A most wicked Sir Oliver, Audrey, a most
vile Martext. But, Audrey, there is a youth here in the
forest lays claim to you.

8   AUDREY   Ay, I know who 'tis. He hath no interest in me
in the world. Here comes the man you mean.
Enter William.

10   TOUCHSTONE   It is meat and drink to me to see a clown;
by my troth, we that have good wits have much to an-
12   swer for. We shall be flouting; we cannot hold.

WILLIAM   Good ev'n, Audrey.

14   AUDREY   God ye good ev'n, William.

WILLIAM   And good ev'n to you, sir.

16   TOUCHSTONE   Good ev'n, gentle friend. Cover thy head,
cover thy head. Nay, prithee be covered. How old are
you, friend?

WILLIAM   Five and twenty, sir.

20   TOUCHSTONE   A ripe age. Is thy name William?

V.1 The forest   **8** *interest in* right or title to   **10** *clown* (1) a person from the
country, (2) a bumpkin   **12** *flouting* mocking; *hold* i.e., hold our tongues
14 *God ye* God give you   **16** *Cover thy head* (out of respect, William has
taken his hat off)

WILLIAM   William, sir.

TOUCHSTONE   A fair name. Wast born i' th' forest here?

WILLIAM   Ay, sir, I thank God.

TOUCHSTONE   "Thank God." A good answer. Art rich?

WILLIAM   Fair, sir, so-so.

TOUCHSTONE   "So-so" is good, very good, very excellent
good; and yet it is not, it is but so-so. Art thou wise?

WILLIAM   Ay, sir, I have a pretty wit.

TOUCHSTONE   Why, thou sayest well. I do now remem-   30
ber a saying, "The fool doth think he is wise, but the
wise man knows himself to be a fool." The heathen
philosopher, when he had a desire to eat a grape, would
open his lips when he put it into his mouth, meaning
thereby that grapes were made to eat and lips to open.
You do love this maid?

WILLIAM   I do, sir.

TOUCHSTONE   Give me your hand. Art thou learned?

WILLIAM   No, sir.

TOUCHSTONE   Then learn this of me: to have is to have;
for it is a figure in rhetoric that drink, being poured out   40
of a cup into a glass, by filling the one doth empty the
other; for all your writers do consent that *ipse* is he.   42
Now, you are not *ipse,* for I am he.

WILLIAM   Which he, sir?

TOUCHSTONE   He, sir, that must marry this woman.
Therefore, you clown, abandon (which is in the vulgar,
leave) the society (which in the boorish is, company) of
this female (which in the common is, woman); which
together is, abandon the society of this female, or,
clown, thou perishest; or, to thy better understanding,   50
diest; or, to wit, I kill thee, make thee away, translate
thy life into death, thy liberty into bondage. I will deal

40 *figure in rhetoric* common figure of speech   42 *for . . . he* (authorities all
agree that *ipse* translates as "he himself"; this Latin word was often used to
refer to a successful lover as the very or chosen man)

53 in poison with thee, or in bastinado, or in steel; I will
54 bandy with thee in faction; I will o'errun thee with pol-
    icy; I will kill thee a hundred and fifty ways. Therefore
    tremble and depart.

AUDREY Do, good William.

WILLIAM God rest you, merry sir.   *Exit.*

    Enter Corin.

CORIN Our master and mistress seeks you. Come away,
60 away!

61 TOUCHSTONE Trip, Audrey, trip, Audrey. I attend, I at-
    tend.   *Exeunt.*

                        *

⌘ **V.2** *Enter Orlando and Oliver.*

ORLANDO Is't possible that on so little acquaintance you
    should like her? that but seeing, you should love her?
    and loving, woo? and wooing, she should grant? And
    will you persever to enjoy her?

5 OLIVER Neither call the giddiness of it in question, the
    poverty of her, the small acquaintance, my sudden
    wooing, nor her sudden consenting; but say with me, I
    love Aliena; say with her that she loves me; consent
    with both that we may enjoy each other. It shall be to
10 your good; for my father's house, and all the revenue
11 that was old Sir Rowland's, will I estate upon you, and
    here live and die a shepherd.

    Enter Rosalind [dressed as Ganymede].

ORLANDO You have my consent. Let your wedding be
    tomorrow: thither will I invite the duke and all's con-
    tented followers. Go you and prepare Aliena; for look
    you, here comes my Rosalind.

---

53 *bastinado* beating with sticks   54 *bandy . . . faction* engage in controversy
with you   54–55 *o'errun . . . policy* overwhelm you with cunning   61 *Trip*
move quickly
  V.2 The forest   5 *Neither . . . question* do not raise questions about the
speed of it   11 *estate* settle

ROSALIND   God save you, brother.   17
OLIVER   And you, fair sister.   *[Exit.]*   18
ROSALIND   O my dear Orlando, how it grieves me to see
thee wear thy heart in a scarf!   20
ORLANDO   It is my arm.
ROSALIND   I thought thy heart had been wounded with
the claws of a lion.
ORLANDO   Wounded it is, but with the eyes of a lady.
ROSALIND   Did your brother tell you how I counterfeited
to swoon when he showed me your handkerchief?
ORLANDO   Ay, and greater wonders than that.
ROSALIND   O, I know where you are! Nay, 'tis true. There
was never anything so sudden but the fight of two rams
and Caesar's thrasonical brag of "I came, saw, and over-   30
came"; for your brother and my sister no sooner met
but they looked; no sooner looked but they loved; no
sooner loved but they sighed; no sooner sighed but they
asked one another the reason; no sooner knew the reason but they sought the remedy: and in these degrees   35
have they made a pair of stairs to marriage, which they   36
will climb incontinent, or else be incontinent before   37
marriage: they are in the very wrath of love, and they   38
will together; clubs cannot part them.   39
ORLANDO   They shall be married tomorrow, and I will   40
bid the duke to the nuptial. But, O, how bitter a thing
it is to look into happiness through another man's eyes!
By so much the more shall I tomorrow be at the height
of heart-heaviness, by how much I shall think my
brother happy in having what he wishes for.

---

17 *brother* prospective brother-in-law   18 *sister* (although Rosalind is still
dressed like a man, Oliver addresses her as Orlando does, as "Rosalind," who
would be his prospective sister-in-law)   20 *scarf* sling   30 *thrasonical* boast-
ful (like the braggart soldier Thraso, in Terence's comedy *Eunuchus*)   30–31
"*I . . . overcame*" (Caesar's famous summary of military victory)   35 *degrees*
escalating stages   36 *pair* flight   37 *incontinent . . . incontinent* immediately . . . sexually unrestrained   38 *wrath* passion   39 *clubs* (commonly
used to part combatants)

ROSALIND   Why then, tomorrow I cannot serve your turn for Rosalind?

ORLANDO   I can live no longer by thinking.

ROSALIND   I will weary you then no longer with idle talk-
50   ing. Know of me then, for now I speak to some pur-
51   pose, that I know you are a gentleman of good conceit.
      I speak not this that you should bear a good opinion of
53   my knowledge, insomuch I say I know you are; neither
      do I labor for a greater esteem than may in some little
55   measure draw a belief from you, to do yourself good,
56   and not to grace me. Believe then, if you please, that I
      can do strange things. I have, since I was three year
58   old, conversed with a magician, most profound in his
59   art and yet not damnable. If you do love Rosalind so
60   near the heart as your gesture cries it out, when your
      brother marries Aliena shall you marry her. I know into
      what straits of fortune she is driven; and it is not im-
63   possible to me, if it appear not inconvenient to you, to
      set her before your eyes tomorrow, human as she is, and
      without any danger.

ORLANDO   Speakest thou in sober meanings?

67 ROSALIND   By my life, I do, which I tender dearly,
      though I say I am a magician. Therefore put you in
69   your best array, bid your friends; for if you will be mar-
70   ried tomorrow, you shall; and to Rosalind, if you will.

      Enter Silvius and Phebe.

      Look, here comes a lover of mine and a lover of hers.

PHEBE
      Youth, you have done me much ungentleness
      To show the letter that I writ to you.

----

51 *conceit* intelligence   53 *insomuch* inasmuch as   55 *belief* i.e., confidence in my ability   56 *grace me* bring favor on myself   58 *conversed* had dealings   59 *not damnable* not practicing black magic   60 *gesture . . . out* behavior proclaims   63 *inconvenient* inappropriate   67 *tender* value (the practice of magic was a capital offense; Rosalind is slyly admitting that she is not truly a magician)   69 *bid* invite

ROSALIND
> I care not if I have. It is my study   74
> To seem despiteful and ungentle to you.   75
> You are there followed by a faithful shepherd:
> Look upon him, love him; he worships you.

PHEBE
> Good shepherd, tell this youth what 'tis to love.

SILVIUS
> It is to be all made of sighs and tears;
> And so am I for Phebe.   80

PHEBE   And I for Ganymede.

ORLANDO   And I for Rosalind.

ROSALIND   And I for no woman.

SILVIUS
> It is to be all made of faith and service;
> And so am I for Phebe.

PHEBE   And I for Ganymede.

ORLANDO   And I for Rosalind.

ROSALIND   And I for no woman.

SILVIUS
> It is to be all made of fantasy,
> All made of passion, and all made of wishes,   90
> All adoration, duty, and observance,   91
> All humbleness, all patience, and impatience,
> All purity, all trial, all observance;   93
> And so am I for Phebe.

PHEBE   And so am I for Ganymede.

ORLANDO   And so am I for Rosalind.

ROSALIND   And so am I for no woman.

PHEBE   *[To Rosalind]*
> If this be so, why blame you me to love you?

SILVIUS   *[To Phebe]*
> If this be so, why blame you me to love you?

---

74 *study* conscious endeavor 75 *despiteful* contemptuous 91 *observance* devotion 93 *observance* (many editors, assuming a compositor's error from two lines above, emend this to "obedience")

ORLANDO
100 If this be so, why blame you me to love you?
ROSALIND   Why do you speak too, "Why blame you me
to love you?"
ORLANDO
To her that is not here, nor doth not hear.
104 ROSALIND   Pray you, no more of this; 'tis like the howling of Irish wolves against the moon. *[To Silvius]* I will
help you if I can. *[To Phebe]* I would love you if I could.
Tomorrow meet me all together. *[To Phebe]* I will marry
you if ever I marry woman, and I'll be married tomor-
109 row. *[To Orlando]* I will satisfy you if ever I satisfied
110 man, and you shall be married tomorrow. *[To Silvius]* I
will content you if what pleases you contents you, and
you shall be married tomorrow. *[To Orlando]* As you
love Rosalind, meet. *[To Silvius]* As you love Phebe,
meet. And as I love no woman, I'll meet. So fare you
well. I have left you commands.
SILVIUS   I'll not fail if I live.
PHEBE   Nor I.
ORLANDO   Nor I.   *Exeunt.*

*

∾ V.3 *Enter [Touchstone the] Clown and Audrey.*

TOUCHSTONE   Tomorrow is the joyful day, Audrey; tomorrow will we be married.
AUDREY   I do desire it with all my heart; and I hope it is
4 no dishonest desire to desire to be a woman of the
world. Here come two of the banished duke's pages.

___
104–5 *like . . . moon* (then as now, howling at the moon was considered a
passionate but pointless way of expressing feeling; since the Irish were often
associated with disorder and savagery, Irish wolves might be considered especially rowdy yet ineffectual)   109 *satisfied* (some editors emend this to "satisfy" on the assumption that Rosalind has never yet satisfied a man)
   V.3 The forest   4 *dishonest* immodest   4–5 *to be . . . world* to be married
(and also to go beyond her present rustic station in life)

Enter two Pages.

FIRST PAGE   Well met, honest gentleman.

TOUCHSTONE   By my troth, well met. Come, sit, sit, and
a song!

SECOND PAGE   We are for you. Sit i' th' middle.   9

FIRST PAGE   Shall we clap into't roundly, without hawk-   10
ing or spitting or saying we are hoarse, which are the
only prologues to a bad voice?   12

SECOND PAGE   I' faith, i' faith! and both in a tune, like   13
two gypsies on a horse.

[Both Pages sing.]

> It was a lover and his lass,
>   With a hey, and a ho, and a hey nonino,
> That o'er the green cornfield did pass   17
>   In springtime, the only pretty ringtime,   18
> When birds do sing, hey ding a ding, ding.
> Sweet lovers love the spring.   20
>
> Between the acres of the rye,
>   With a hey, and a ho, and a hey nonino,
> These pretty country folks would lie
>   In springtime, etc.
>
> This carol they began that hour,
>   With a hey, and a ho, and a hey nonino,
> How that a life was but a flower
>   In springtime, etc.
>
> And therefore take the present time,   29
>   With a hey, and a ho, and a hey nonino,   30
> For love is crownèd with the prime   31
>   In springtime, etc.

---

9 *for you* ready for you   10 *clap into't roundly* start right off   12 *only* common   13 *in a tune* in unison   17 *cornfield* wheat field   18 *ringtime* wedding
season   29 *take . . . time* seize the moment   31 *prime* spring

TOUCHSTONE Truly, young gentlemen, though there
34   was no great matter in the ditty, yet the note was very
35   untuneable.

FIRST PAGE   You are deceived, sir. We kept time, we lost
not our time.

TOUCHSTONE   By my troth, yes; I count it but time lost
to hear such a foolish song. God b' wi' you, and God
40   mend your voices. Come, Audrey.   *Exeunt.*

*

∾ **V.4** *Enter Duke Senior, Amiens, Jaques, Orlando,
Oliver, Celia [dressed as Aliena].*

DUKE SENIOR
   Dost thou believe, Orlando, that the boy
   Can do all this that he hath promisèd?

ORLANDO
   I sometimes do believe, and sometimes do not,
4   As those that fear they hope, and know they fear.
      *Enter Rosalind [dressed as Ganymede], Silvius, and
      Phebe.*

ROSALIND
5   Patience once more, whiles our compact is urged.
   You say, if I bring in your Rosalind,
   You will bestow her on Orlando here?

DUKE SENIOR
   That would I, had I kingdoms to give with her.

ROSALIND
   And you say you will have her when I bring her?

ORLANDO
10   That would I, were I of all kingdoms king.

ROSALIND
   You say you'll marry me, if I be willing?

---

34 *matter* substance 35 *untuneable* off key
   V.4 The forest 4 *fear they hope* i.e., fear they hope only fruitlessly 5
compact contract; *urged* proclaimed

PHEBE
    That will I, should I die the hour after.
ROSALIND
    But if you do refuse to marry me,
    You'll give yourself to this most faithful shepherd?
PHEBE
    So is the bargain.
ROSALIND
    You say that you'll have Phebe, if she will?
SILVIUS
    Though to have her and death were both one thing.   17
ROSALIND
    I have promised to make all this matter even.   18
    Keep you your word, O duke, to give your daughter;
    You yours, Orlando, to receive his daughter;   20
    Keep you your word, Phebe, that you'll marry me,
    Or else, refusing me, to wed this shepherd;
    Keep your word, Silvius, that you'll marry her
    If she refuse me; and from hence I go,
    To make these doubts all even.   25
                    Exeunt Rosalind and Celia.
DUKE SENIOR
    I do remember in this shepherd boy
    Some lively touches of my daughter's favor.   27
ORLANDO
    My lord, the first time that I ever saw him
    Methought he was a brother to your daughter.
    But, my good lord, this boy is forest-born,   30
    And hath been tutored in the rudiments
    Of many desperate studies by his uncle,   32
    Whom he reports to be a great magician,
    Obscurèd in the circle of this forest.   34
        Enter [Touchstone the] Clown and Audrey.

---

17 *both . . . thing* the same   18 *even* plain   25 *make . . . even* clear up your
misgivings   27 *lively* lifelike; *favor* appearance   32 *desperate* dangerous   34
Obscurèd hidden

35 JAQUES There is, sure, another flood toward, and these
      couples are coming to the ark. Here comes a pair of
      very strange beasts, which in all tongues are called
      fools.

    TOUCHSTONE Salutation and greeting to you all!

40 JAQUES Good my lord, bid him welcome. This is the
      motley-minded gentleman that I have so often met in
      the forest. He hath been a courtier, he swears.

    TOUCHSTONE If any man doubt that, let him put me to
44   my purgation. I have trod a measure; I have flattered a
      lady; I have been politic with my friend, smooth with
46   mine enemy; I have undone three tailors; I have had
47   four quarrels, and like to have fought one.

48 JAQUES And how was that ta'en up?

    TOUCHSTONE Faith, we met, and found the quarrel was
50   upon the seventh cause.

    JAQUES How seventh cause? Good my lord, like this fel-
      low.

    DUKE SENIOR I like him very well.

54 TOUCHSTONE God 'ild you, sir; I desire you of the like.
55   I press in here, sir, amongst the rest of the country cop-
      ulatives, to swear and to forswear, according as mar-
57   riage binds and blood breaks. A poor virgin, sir, an
58   ill-favored thing, sir, but mine own; a poor humor of
59   mine, sir, to take that that no man else will. Rich hon-
60   esty dwells like a miser, sir, in a poor house, as your
      pearl in your foul oyster.

62 DUKE SENIOR By my faith, he is very swift and senten-
      tious.

---

35 *toward* approaching 35–36 *these couples . . . ark* (see Genesis 7:2, where
pairs of male and female animals board Noah's ark to escape the flood and to
repopulate the earth after the waters subside) 44 *purgation* trial, proof;
measure dance 46 *undone* ruined 47 *like to have* almost 48 *ta'en up* settled 54 *'ild* reward; *I desire . . . like* I wish you the same compliment
55–56 *copulatives* i.e., those about to couple 57 *blood* passion; *breaks* breaks
up or out 58 *humor* eccentricity 59–60 *honesty* chastity 62–63 *senten-
tious* full of pithy sayings or proverbial wisdom

TOUCHSTONE According to the fool's bolt, sir, and such   64
dulcet diseases.   65

JAQUES But, for the seventh cause. How did you find the
quarrel on the seventh cause?

TOUCHSTONE Upon a lie seven times removed (bear
your body more seeming, Audrey) as thus, sir. I did dis- 69
like the cut of a certain courtier's beard. He sent me   70
word, if I said his beard was not cut well, he was in the
mind it was: this is called the Retort Courteous. If I
sent him word again it was not well cut, he would send
me word he cut it to please himself: this is called the
Quip Modest. If again, it was not well cut, he disabled   75
my judgment: this is called the Reply Churlish. If
again, it was not well cut, he would answer I spake not
true: this is called the Reproof Valiant. If again, it was
not well cut, he would say I lie: this is called the Coun- 79
tercheck Quarrelsome; and so to the Lie Circumstan-   80
tial and the Lie Direct.

JAQUES And how oft did you say his beard was not well
cut?

TOUCHSTONE I durst go no further than the Lie Circumstantial, nor he durst not give me the Lie Direct;
and so we measured swords and parted.   86

JAQUES Can you nominate in order now the degrees of   87
the lie?

TOUCHSTONE O sir, we quarrel in print, by the book, as   89
you have books for good manners. I will name you the   90
degrees. The first, the Retort Courteous; the second,
the Quip Modest; the third, the Reply Churlish; the
fourth, the Reproof Valiant; the fifth, the Coun-

---

64 *bolt* arrow (which is quickly shot)   65 *dulcet diseases* pleasant afflictions
69 *seeming* (1) modestly, (2) attractively   69–70 *dislike* criticize   69–81
I . . . Direct (Touchstone ridicules the etiquette of quarreling, which he has
learned from books)   75 *Modest* moderate; *disabled* disqualified   79–80
Countercheck contradiction   80–81 *Circumstantial* indirect   86 *measured
swords* ensured that their swords were the same length, as if they were prepar-
ing for a duel   87 *nominate* name   89 *by the book* according to the rules

94   tercheck Quarrelsome; the sixth, the Lie with Circum-
      stance; the seventh, the Lie Direct. All these you may
      avoid but the Lie Direct, and you may avoid that too,
97   with an If. I knew when seven justices could not take
      up a quarrel, but when the parties were met themselves,
      one of them thought but of an If: as, "If you said so,
100   then I said so"; and they shook hands and swore broth-
      ers. Your If is the only peacemaker. Much virtue in If.
      JAQUES   Is not this a rare fellow, my lord? He's as good at
      anything, and yet a fool.
104   DUKE SENIOR   He uses his folly like a stalking horse, and
105   under the presentation of that he shoots his wit.
           Enter Hymen, [and] Rosalind and Celia [dressed as
           themselves]. Still music.

      HYMEN
           Then is there mirth in heaven
107   When earthly things made even
108   Atone together.
           Good duke, receive thy daughter;
110   Hymen from heaven brought her,
               Yea, brought her hither,
112   That thou mightst join his hand with his
           Whose heart within his bosom is.
      ROSALIND   *[To the Duke]*
      To you I give myself, for I am yours.
           [To Orlando]
      To you I give myself, for I am yours.

_____

94–95 *with Circumstance* i.e., only circumstantial, indirect   97–98 *take up*
settle   100–1 *swore brothers* swore themselves brothers   104 *stalking horse* any
object used to hide a hunter stalking game   105 *under . . . that* i.e., while
using the guise of his folly; **s.d.** *Hymen* the god of marriage in classical myth;
Still soft   107 *made even* set to rights   108 *Atone* are brought into balance or
united   112 *his hand* (Editors routinely emend this to "her hand." Yet *his* suggests that Rosalind's masculine identity as Ganymede lingers here. Orlando is
joined to her, but also to him.)

DUKE SENIOR
  If there be truth in sight, you are my daughter.   116
ORLANDO
  If there be truth in sight, you are my Rosalind.
PHEBE
  If sight and shape be true,
  Why then, my love adieu!
ROSALIND   *[To the Duke]*
  I'll have no father, if you be not he.   120
      [To Orlando]
  I'll have no husband, if you be not he.
      [To Phebe]
  Nor ne'er wed woman, if you be not she.

HYMEN
              Peace ho! I bar confusion:
              'Tis I must make conclusion
                  Of these most strange events.
              Here's eight that must take hands
              To join in Hymen's bands,
                  If truth holds true contents.   128
      [To Orlando and Rosalind]
              You and you no cross shall part.   129
      [To Oliver and Celia]
              You and you are heart in heart.   130
      [To Phebe]
              You to his love must accord,   131
              Or have a woman to your lord.
      [To Touchstone and Audrey]
              You and you are sure together   133
              As the winter to foul weather.

---

116 *If . . . sight* i.e., if my eyes do not deceive me   128 *If . . . contents* i.e., if
the discoveries made by the couples reveal their genuine affections   129 *cross*
disagreement   131 *accord* assent   133 *sure together* securely united

[To all]
Whiles a wedlock hymn we sing,
136   Feed yourselves with questioning,
137   That reason wonder may diminish
How thus we met, and these things finish.
[All sing.]
139   Wedding is great Juno's crown,
140   O blessed bond of board and bed!
'Tis Hymen peoples every town;
High wedlock then be honorèd.
Honor, high honor, and renown
To Hymen, god of every town!

DUKE SENIOR
O my dear niece, welcome thou art to me,
146   Even daughter, welcome, in no less degree!

PHEBE   *[To Silvius]*
I will not eat my word, now thou art mine;
148   Thy faith my fancy to thee doth combine.
Enter [Jaques de Boys].

JAQUES DE BOYS
Let me have audience for a word or two.
150   I am the second son of old Sir Rowland
That bring these tidings to this fair assembly.
Duke Frederick, hearing how that every day
Men of great worth resorted to this forest,
154   Addressed a mighty power, which were on foot
155   In his own conduct, purposely to take

---

136 *Feed* satisfy   137 *reason* understanding   139 *Juno* goddess of marriage
140 *board* table (legal and popular discussions of marriage focused on the
dining table and the bed as the most important sites of domestic life)   146
Even daughter just as if you were my daughter   148 *fancy* desire, love; *combine* unite   s.d. *Jaques de Boys* i.e., the brother to Oliver and Orlando   154
Addressed assembled; *power* force (of troops)   155 *In . . . conduct* under his
own command

His brother here and put him to the sword;
And to the skirts of this wild wood he came,   157
Where, meeting with an old religious man,
After some question with him, was converted   159
Both from his enterprise and from the world,   160
His crown bequeathing to his banished brother,
And all their lands restored to them again
That were with him exiled. This to be true
I do engage my life.   164
DUKE SENIOR   Welcome, young man.
Thou offer'st fairly to thy brothers' wedding: 165
To one, his lands withheld; and to the other,
A land itself at large, a potent dukedom.
First, in this forest let us do those ends   168
That here were well begun and well begot;
And after, every of this happy number   170
That have endured shrewd days and nights with us   171
Shall share the good of our returnèd fortune,
According to the measure of their states.   173
Meantime forget this new-fall'n dignity   174
And fall into our rustic revelry.
Play, music, and you brides and bridegrooms all,
With measure heaped in joy, to th' measures fall.   177
JAQUES
Sir, by your patience. If I heard you rightly,   178
The duke hath put on a religious life   179
And thrown into neglect the pompous court.   180
JAQUES DE BOYS   He hath.
JAQUES
To him will I. Out of these convertites   182

---

157 *skirts* outskirts 159 *question* discussion 164 *engage* pledge 165 *Thou . . . fairly* you bring rich gifts 168 *do those ends* complete those purposes 170 *every* every one 171 *shrewd* evil 173 *states* i.e., status 174 *new-fall'n* newly acquired 177 *measure* portion; *measures* dances (with a full portion of joy, start dancing) 178 *by your patience* with your permission 179 *put . . . life* adopted the life of a monk or hermit 180 *pompous* ostentatious, consumed with ceremony 182 *convertites* converts

There is much matter to be heard and learned.
        [To the Duke]
You to your former honor I bequeath;
Your patience and your virtue well deserves it.
        [To Orlando]
You to a love that your true faith doth merit;
        [To Oliver]
You to your land and love and great allies;
        [To Silvius]
188 You to a long and well-deservèd bed;
        [To Touchstone]
And you to wrangling, for thy loving voyage
190 Is but for two months victualled. So, to your pleasures:
I am for other than for dancing measures.
DUKE SENIOR   Stay, Jaques, stay.
JAQUES
193 To see no pastime I. What you would have
I'll stay to know at your abandoned cave.   *Exit.*
DUKE SENIOR
Proceed, proceed. We'll begin these rites,
As we do trust they'll end, in true delights.
                                        Exit [in the dance].

[EPILOGUE]

1 ROSALIND   It is not the fashion to see the lady the epi-
2   logue, but it is no more unhandsome than to see the
     lord the prologue. If it be true that good wine needs no
3   bush, 'tis true that a good play needs no epilogue; yet to
     good wine they do use good bushes, and good plays

---

188 *long* long-lasting   190 *victualled* supplied with food   193 *What . . .
have* what you want from me
    Epilogue   1 *the lady* i.e., the actor playing the play's heroine   **2** *unhand-
some* unbecoming   **3** *bush* ivy bush (i.e., promotion; taverns customarily
hung out a branch of ivy to show that wine was for sale within)

prove the better by the help of good epilogues. What a   6
case am I in then, that am neither a good epilogue, nor
cannot insinuate with you in the behalf of a good play!   8
I am not furnished like a beggar; therefore to beg will   9
not become me. My way is to conjure you, and I'll   10
begin with the women. I charge you, O women, for the
love you bear to men, to like as much of this play as   12
please you; and I charge you, O men, for the love you
bear to women (as I perceive by your simpering none of
you hates them), that between you and the women the
play may please. If I were a woman, I would kiss as   16
many of you as had beards that pleased me, complex-
ions that liked me, and breaths that I defied not; and I   18
am sure, as many as have good beards, or good faces, or
sweet breaths, will, for my kind offer, when I make   20
curtsy, bid me farewell.   *Exit.*   21

---

6 *case* predicament 8 *insinuate* ingratiate myself 9 *furnished* equipped
(i.e., with rags and a cup) 10 *conjure* urge, enchant 12 *like* (a reminder of
the play's title); *please* may please 16 *If . . . woman* (a reminder that the
actor was a boy) 18 *liked* pleased; *defied* rejected 21 *bid me farewell* i.e.,
with applause

The distinguished Pelican Shakespeare series, newly revised
to be the premier choice for students, professors, and
general readers well into the 21st century

All's Well That Ends Well
ISBN 0-14-071460-X

Antony and Cleopatra
ISBN 0-14-071452-9

As You Like It
ISBN 0-14-071471-5

The Comedy of Errors
ISBN 0-14-071474-X

Coriolanus
ISBN 0-14-071473-1

Cymbeline
ISBN 0-14-071472-3

Hamlet
ISBN 0-14-071454-5

Henry IV, Part I
ISBN 0-14-071456-1

Henry IV, Part 2
ISBN 0-14-071457-X

Henry V
ISBN 0-14-071458-8

Henry VI, Part 1
ISBN 0-14-071465-0

Henry VI, Part 2
ISBN 0-14-071466-9

Henry VI, Part 3
ISBN 0-14-071467-7

Henry VIII
ISBN 0-14-071475-8

Julius Caesar
ISBN 0-14-071468-5

King John
ISBN 0-14-071459-6

King Lear
ISBN 0-14-071476-6

King Lear
(The Quarto and Folio Texts)
ISBN 0-14-071490-1

Love's Labor's Lost
ISBN 0-14-071477-4

Macbeth
ISBN 0-14-071478-2

FOR THE BEST IN PAPERBACKS, LOOK FOR THE

Measure for Measure
ISBN 0-14-071479-0

The Merchant of Venice
ISBN 0-14-071462-6

The Merry Wives of Windsor
ISBN 0-14-071464-2

A Midsummer Night's Dream
ISBN 0-14-071455-3

Much Ado About Nothing
ISBN 0-14-071480-4

The Narrative Poems
ISBN 0-14-071481-2

Othello
ISBN 0-14-071463-4

Pericles
ISBN 0-14-071469-3

Richard II
ISBN 0-14-071482-0

Richard III
ISBN 0-14-071483-9

Romeo and Juliet
ISBN 0-14-071484-7

The Sonnets
ISBN 0-14-071453-7

The Taming of the Shrew
ISBN 0-14-071451-0

The Tempest
ISBN 0-14-071485-5

Timon of Athens
ISBN 0-14-071487-1

Titus Andronicus
ISBN 0-14-071491-X

Troilus and Cressida
ISBN 0-14-071486-3

Twelfth Night
ISBN 0-14-071489-8

The Two Gentlemen of Verona
ISBN 0-14-071461-8

The Winter's Tale
ISBN 0-14-071488-X

AVAILABLE FROM PENGUIN CLASSICS

THE PELICAN SHAKESPEARE

Hamlet • King Lear • Macbeth

A Midsummer Night's Dream • Romeo and Juliet • Twelfth Night

General Editors: Stephen Orgel and A. R. Braunmuller

New Illustrated Covers designed by Manuja Waldia